For Both the Family and The Business!

SAY ANYTHING

How Leaders Inspire Ideas, Cultivate
Candor, and Forge Fearless Cultures

by Doug Crandall & Matt Kincaid, PhD

INSPIRE: to draw forth or bring out

CULTIVATE: to foster the growth of

FORGE: to form or bring into being
especially by an expenditure of effort

Published in the United States by Blue Rudder Leadership
Seattle, WA
www.bluerudderleadership.com
www.sayanythingleadership.com

"Funded with Kickstarter" and K logos are trademarks of
Kickstarter, Inc. Use does not imply endorsement.

Edited by Joanie Eppinga, Spokane, WA

Library of Congress Cataloging-in-Publication Data
Crandall, Doug and Kincaid, Matt, PhD
     Say Anything: How Leaders Inspire Ideas, Cultivate
Candor and Forge Fearless Cultures / Doug Crandall and Matt
Kincaid, PhD.
p. cm.

Includes bibliographical references and index.
1. Business Management—Leadership. 2. Organizational Culture—
Leadership. 3. Communication—Leadership. 4. Interpersonal Relations
—Psychological Aspects. I. Title
2014919664
ISBN 978-1502344199

Printed in the United States of America
10 9 8 7 6 5 4 3 2

First Edition

"Crandall and Kincaid make these rare leadership concepts accessible, interesting, and understandable. SAY ANYTHING challenges you to listen, learn, and lead with enthusiasm and respect for everyone on your team. It's a quick and important read—relevant to successful healthcare leaders everywhere."

Kate Walsh, CEO, Boston Medical Center

"At Proactive Coaching, we work with some of the best teams and coaches in the world. SAY ANYTHING will be this year's #1 recommendation for all of them. It should be in the hands—and hearts and minds—of every executive, teacher, administrator, or coach who wants to earn trust and build a winning team."

Bruce Brown, Proactive Coaching

"Crandall and Kincaid adroitly reveal how leaders inadvertently derail creativity and commitment, and deliver keen insights on how to avoid that trap. SAY ANYTHING is a powerful reminder to leaders they aren't necessarily the smartest people in the room."

Tom Kolditz, Yale School of Management

funded with
KICK STARTER

We set out to write a book with wide reach and tremendous impact. But we aspired to do it in a grassroots way. In mid-October of 2014, we reached our crowdfunding goal with the help of one hundred and sixteen generous backers.

We've recognized our major supporters below. Thank you!

Bill Bishop	Kim Baldwin
Mary Kincaid	Sean Myers
Erik Egger	Brad Edwards
The Boda Group	Everett Spain
Brian McConnell	Jennifer Jahner
David Orton	Jason Elk
Trent Miller	Michael Ochs
Sam Deen	Tom Pae
Suzanne Franklin	Jessica Shoup McConnell
Mariellen Johnson	James Gonzalez
Greg and Kristin Duff	Amber Ballard Dossey
Mark Schuster	Deb Alley
Grant Ries	Geoff and Sarah Webb
Vik Bhatia	Aaron Kohler
Kevin Crawford	Andrew Halvorson
Lori Carson-Chafe	Sarah Kincaid Rapoza
Kirt Shaffer	Jennifer Anderson
Richard Cummins	Joanne Crandall
Stephen Lasslo	Shann Ferch
Jeff Richards	Jim Draudt

And special thanks to Backer #1: Amanda Axelson

CONTENTS

Foreword by Jennifer Porter

Author's Note by Matt Kincaid

THE PROBLEM

1. THE RIGHT DECISION...a surprising display of candor in an NFL playoff game introduces the power of Say Anything leadership.

2. ANOTHER OPTION...the push and pull of competing interests stymies a rising star. What if he had another option? An overview of SAY ANYTHING.

3. IN THE TANK...an illuminating experience on a reality television show introduces the debilitating impact of power, past experiences, and fear.

THE DYNAMICS

4. SUFFOCATING POWER...a mystery, co-pilots, and a nuclear submarine demonstrate how leaders talk too much and power suffocates ideas.

5. ONCE BITTEN...a pre-school teacher, nurses, and an external hire highlight how the pain of past experiences keeps quiet those you lead.

11. DIGNIFY EVERY TRY...once it's safe, people will speak up. A renowned horse whisperer shares the magic of honoring every try: from a new drink idea to a really bad NBA trade proposal.

12. BE GENUINELY CURIOUS...one of the world's most powerful women, redwood tress, and an apple orchard teach us to listen to all, never drop anchor, and ask Authentic Questions.

IN CONCLUSION

After all this, we hope you'll be equipped and inspired to head for...

13. THE PROMISED LAND...a portrait of what it looks like when leaders forge a truly fearless culture: teenage girls call it like they see it and employee engagement sets a global benchmark.

EXTRA: REFLECTION AND ACTION...a small package of reflection questions, notes, tools, and further learning to help leaders inspire ideas, cultivate candor, and forge fearless cultures.

FOREWORD

In March of 2014, Doug and I were in Paris working with the extended leadership team of a global technology company—guiding them through a discussion about leadership and how to navigate substantial strategic changes in their organization. It wasn't going well. The leaders in the room exhibited varying levels of engagement, were not listening to one another, and many didn't think "leadership" was all that important to their company's success. At a break, Doug looked at me, exasperated, and said, "They don't get it. Leadership is about *taking care of people*. They may never hire us again, but they need to take a harder look. I've got to say it." Doug and Matt don't just preach what's inside this book, they do it every day. And more important, they teach leaders how to cultivate such candor in members of their teams. This game-changing book will now help a broader set of leaders do the same.

The core message of SAY ANYTHING is this: as leaders, it's entirely **our** responsibility to create an environment that supports and encourages candor and fearlessness. This includes demonstrating the behavior ourselves, making it safe for those we lead to speak up, dignifying every effort, and being genuinely curious when people Say Anything to us. It sounds so simple, and yet very few leaders do this.

I've been an executive coach for over a decade. I've helped develop hundreds of leaders and leadership teams and have come to realize the single biggest challenge leaders face is empowering those inside their organizations to Say Anything—to bring forth every idea, to talk candidly about how they are working together, to give each other thoughtful and constructive feedback, to process truthfully what is happening and how to make it better. We've seen it over and over again. Colleagues gather around literal and figurative water coolers and say privately what they won't say publicly. They are afraid to share their perspectives and have learned to either keep their mouth shut or to share their ideas with people other than those who need to hear them. Leaders tell us, "We have have an amazing team. There's no conflict. We're all on the same page." And then team members tell us they're leaving the organization because it's not on track; they don't believe they can speak up; the team isn't aligned; the leader doesn't listen; nothing will ever change; or they've tried to speak up and been smacked down or punished.

SAY ANYTHING caused me to take pause, reflect, and notice the places I am doing well and places where I am falling short. I'm already better for it. You will be too.

Jennifer Porter
The Boda Group
Boston, MA

AUTHOR'S NOTE

Co-authoring a book brings with it two life stories, two interpretations of research, two opinions, and perhaps most challenging, two voices. For many years Doug and I [Matt] have studied successful examples of co-authored books from our industry. Authors like Barry Posner and Jim Kouzes, and brothers Chip and Dan Heath, do a beautiful job using a "we" approach and maintaining a singular voice throughout their work. We began this book with this idea in mind—one uniform voice—but realized early on it wasn't going to work well.

One of the most important foundational principles in leader development is authenticity. Exhaustive studies demonstrate that more than anything else, the most effective leaders know who they are and stay tightly fastened to their core values. In other words, the best leaders are authentic and don't put on a mask each day pretending to be someone else. Doug and I work with leaders, in some cases for years at a time, delving into the depths of their personal journeys to discover their most authentic core. This journey—what we call "leading self"—lays the foundation for enhancing leadership of others. We passionately believe in this *inside-out* approach.

As we worked on content for this book, we realized writing the entire narrative using a "we" format would not be authentic. Much of our best supporting content is from Doug's personal life. A "we" voice in a story that is Doug's—when I wasn't even there—is a dishonest representation of both the story and of us. Thus we abandoned the notion of solely using one uniform voice.

So, as you read on, please note the following:

- We use "we" only when it's accurate—primarily when explaining research and conceptual points.
- Any time you read "I", it is Doug's story told in the first-person. His voice is the primary backbone throughout the body of the narrative.
- We toggle back and forth between "we" and "I", as it makes sense.
- We call out "Doug" on occasion to help the story make sense when it is coming from both of us. For instance, you'll see in the *Introduction*: "Doug's wife recommended..."
- We use "Matt" when referring to me—even if the content is a personal story from my life—so as not to be confusing by including a second first-person voice.

One other important point: we believe leadership is best taught by those who have led. Personal stories and examples play a critical role in SAY ANYTHING. But grounded academic theory is also immensely valuable. We've studied extensively the research of Francesca Gino and colleagues, Gary Stasser, Dov Eden, Amy Edmondson, Daniel Kahneman, and many others. This book owes much to their work. On rare occasion, we substitute a word or phrase to clarify context—without changing the true meaning of a passage. We've highlighted these instances in either our footnotes or endnotes. As a result of the attention to both practicality and credibility, we believe you'll find this book a delightful mix of compelling anecdote and solid leadership theory.

Thanks for reading. Enjoy—

Matt Kincaid
Blue Rudder Leadership
Richland, WA

Nothing strengthens authority
so much as silence.
-Leonardo da Vinci

THE PROBLEM

1. THE RIGHT DECISION...

Multipliers don't focus on what they know but on how to know what others know; they are interested in every relevant insight people can offer.
-Liz Wiseman, best-selling author of *Multipliers*

During the 2013 National Football League season, the Seattle Seahawks paid Steven Hauschka $715,000 to kick a football through the uprights when the team needed three points. Hauschka was a worthy employee, successfully converting 33 of his 35 three-point attempts (or $21,666.67 per field goal) during the sixteen-game campaign. His 94.3% success rate in 2013 was eight percentage points higher than his career average and placed him second in NFL field goal accuracy.

Steven Hauschka had never even kicked a football in a competitive setting until the fall of 2004—his third semester at Vermont's Middlebury College. He was cut from the varsity soccer team as a freshman, so at the outset of sophomore year, his roommate urged him to try out for the football team. Middlebury desperately needed a kicker. Hauschka made the team and went on to set numerous records over three years. After finishing up at Middlebury with a degree in neuroscience, he went on to a year of graduate school at North Carolina State, where he also served as the Wolfpack's field goal kicker.

A successful season kicking for a Division I college football program caught the attention of the Minnesota Vikings, who signed Hauschka to its pre-season squad as an undrafted free agent. He didn't make the team, however, and spent the next three years wandering the NFL—including regular and pre-season stints with the Baltimore Ravens, Atlanta Falcons, Detroit Lions, and Denver Broncos. He even logged a season with the Las Vegas Locomotives of the obscure and now-defunct United Football League.

Hauschka's stellar 2013 performance continued into 2014 as the Seattle Seahawks made a run toward the Super Bowl. Early in the 4th quarter of the NFC Championship game versus the San Francisco 49ers, Pete Carroll called on his kicker for a fourth-down, fifty-three-yard field goal that would bring the Seahawks within one point of the lead. The moment was not lost on any Seattle fan. It had been thirty-five years since a major, professional sports team had won a championship for the city. That team—the Seattle SuperSonics of the NBA—was "stolen" by Clay Bennett and moved to Oklahoma City in 2008. By 2014, many in the Pacific Northwest still reeled from the lack of a basketball team. Moreover, the Seattle Mariners had not been to the Major League Baseball playoffs in well over a decade. Seattle ranked with Cleveland and maybe Kansas City as the most tortured sports cities in America. The 2013-2014 Seahawks had a chance to not only win the Super Bowl, but end the long-suffering of an entire region.

Steven Hauschka—the wanderer who had finally found some job security with the Seahawks—was about to trot on the field to execute one of the more important kicks of his career. But as he passed by Pete Carroll, Hauschka noticed the wind marker at the top of the north upright whipping swiftly in a southerly direction. He gave it some quick thought and decided the field goal attempt was not the right decision. This guy, who Seahawks' owner Paul Allen was paying three quarters of a million dollars per year to kick a football, didn't think the field goal try was a good idea. So what did Hauschka do? He buckled down, thought positive, and made the kick...

No. That is *not* what Steven Hauschka did in that moment. Instead, he grabbed his coach and stated plainly: "We shouldn't kick this." He then ran onto the turf and stared at the spot where the football was to be placed. A few seconds later, Pete Carroll called a timeout. From the stands, or the comfort of a living room, it was a curious scene; it even provided an appearance of confusion and indecision. The kicker had taken his spot on the field and waited for the snap and placement of the ball, only to be called back to the sideline.

Pete Carroll had listened. The Seahawks would not have Hauschka attempt a field goal, but instead would go for it on 4th down. A series of events that appeared puzzling to fans in front of television sets would make perfect sense after the game: an employee had provided input into a decision and his leader adjusted course. Hauschka's journey from Middlebury to undrafted free agent to wanderer to somewhat-stable Seahawks employee undoubtedly hovered over his relationship with his boss. He likely felt fortunate to have any job at all. His status as a lowly kicker also weighed in. While important at critical times, field goal specialists are usually low-status members of any NFL team. Pete Carroll's expected response to Steven Hauschka's input?

"I made the call. Just do your job. Kicker."

In fact, direct reports of Carroll—heads about to explode—were standing in earshot of the head coach thinking much worse. One of them could hardly believe Hauschka would even open his mouth. The Seahawks were (over)paying him to do what the coach told him. Carroll, on the other hand, welcomed the candor—especially from the guy who knew this part of the "business" better than anyone else: "I love the honesty. Most guys go and say 'I can make it' and go out there and plunk it down at the goal line. I thought it was a great moment for us, and it was a great decision."

Doug's wife recommended we not begin this book with the Hauschka example. Thousands of San Francisco 49er fans are bound to stop reading, she warned. There are many college football enthusiasts who hate Pete Carroll and think he cheated at USC. People in New York and Boston remember his failed tenures with the Jets and Patriots. But the fact remains: in 2014, Pete Carroll was the overwhelming winner when ESPN asked two hundred and thirty NFL players, "Which head coach would you most like to play for?" Carroll garnered twenty-three percent of the votes, far outpacing Mike Tomlin of the Pittsburgh

Steelers who received fourteen percent. No other head coach reached double digits.

Reflecting on the survey results, Carroll observed, "We're open around here. We're honest enough and straightforward enough that we can talk right to our guys about any issue in front of the rest of the team." Honest enough and open enough that when Steven Hauschka didn't think he would convert a critical field goal attempt, he was willing to say so.

> "I didn't think it was the right decision, and I let Coach Carroll know that."

What happened next is almost secondary to the overall leadership lesson, but the fortunate turn of events makes the anecdote all the more intriguing. Carroll calls timeout. The offense goes back on the field. Hundreds of thousands of fans turn to each other and wonder what's going on. Moments later Russell Wilson throws a thirty-six yard touchdown strike to Jermaine Kearse that gives the Seahawks the lead in the fourth quarter—a lead they would not relinquish. Seahawks fans go wild. 49ers fans shake their heads. Steven Hauschka, lowly kicker—at one of the most critical moments of his career—felt empowered to question his coach's decision. In fact, he didn't just question the decision; he told Pete Carroll it was a not a good idea. Equally important, Carroll listened.

This book is for leaders of any kind. If you are a leader, people will hesitate to say what they think. They will hesitate to question—especially your ideas. They will hesitate to share their own ideas. They will hesitate to ask for help. They will hesitate to point out mistakes and admit mistakes. They will hesitate to call out lapses of integrity. And in many organizations, the hesitation will become suffocation and no one will say anything at all. But study after study pronounces candid communication enhances innovation, ownership, engagement, and overall performance. As Jim Collins observes in his best-selling classic *Good to Great,* "**Leadership is about creating a climate where the truth is heard and the brutal facts are confronted.**"[1]

In February of 2014, the Seattle Seahawks won Super Bowl XLVIII in resounding fashion, bringing the Emerald City its first title in thirty-five years. Over half a million people lined the streets from Key Arena to CenturyLink Field just a few days later. Riding on a Washington National Guard cargo truck, waving to fans stacked ten deep on the sidewalks, Steven Hauschka celebrated with his teammates. He had gone nine for nine during the playoffs. But the most important field goal of the season was probably the one he didn't take. The Seattle Seahawks were Super Bowl champions—in part—because of Steven Hauschka's willingness to **Say Anything** to his head coach. And Pete Carroll was the most popular coach among NFL players—in part

©Zhukovksy

---

[1]"There's a huge difference," Collins points out, "between the opportunity to 'have your say,' and the opportunity to be heard." Pete Carroll undoubtedly heard Hauschka.

—because of the culture he had forged: one of openness and one where he valued the input of every member of the team—even the journeyman kicker.

Counterexamples litter the leadership landscape in iconic form: Watergate, the Space Shuttle disasters, Quaker's $1.4 billion loss on the purchase of Snapple, Jerry Sandusky's crimes at Penn State, a problematic launch of the Obamacare website. In each of these examples, someone either failed to speak up, failed to listen, or both. Silence, or at best timid suggestion, is the norm in most organizations. So how do leaders— real leaders—create an environment where people will Say Anything to each other without fear of reprisal, embarrassment, condemnation, or even rolling eyeballs? How do leaders create a place where team members speak openly, anytime, and all the time?

2. ANOTHER OPTION

No matter what people tell you,
words and ideas can change the world.
-Robin Williams in Dead Poets Society

Jeff Gaines started out as an hourly associate at one of the world's largest retailers. He earned a college degree on the side and then rapidly worked his way through the company's merchandising ranks to become one of its youngest directors. Identified as "top talent," Gaines received a nomination to the company's high-potential leadership program and a promotion to senior director. The original pilot of the leadership development course included an exercise designed to place front-line leaders and headquarters executives in the shoes of their own constituents: The Core Customer Challenge. Because of the emotional impact of the event, it has maintained its place in the curriculum through multiple years of revisions.

Per the challenge, Gaines and his cohort of eight colleagues set out one afternoon to purchase a week's worth of groceries for a family of four. The example family had one five-year-old boy with a gluten intolerance and a newborn baby girl. A dietary specialist gave the group of executives sixty-eight dollars.[2] "Bring back everything the family will need

---

[2] The recommended weekly food allowance for a family just above the poverty line.

to provide three meals per day for a full week," the dietitian directed.

Thirty minutes later, with milk, breakfast cereal, and a loaf of bread loaded in their shopping cart, Jeff Gaines and his group stood in front of the canned vegetables looking for the least expensive offering of green beans. Situated prominently on the middle shelf, the company's private label was the best bargain at sixty-eight cents. A woman on Jeff's team grabbed two cans and tossed them in the cart. Jeff Gaines, though, stopped the group before they could move on. "Just a second," he murmured, "there are some cheaper ones down there."

"Down there" was on the bottom right, out of eyesight for the average-sized human. Jeff spotted the Three Charms brand beans—priced at fifty-two cents per can—because he had put them on the bottom shelf two years earlier while fighting his way up the merchandising ranks as a canned vegetable buyer.[3] When Three Charms came to Jeff with their original pitch, he was hesitant to make the beans part of his assortment. Although doing so would be consistent with company strategy (offering the lowest price point of any retailer) and the company's mission (helping people save money), it conflicted with his own incentive structure. Jeff's target for the year was a four percent revenue increase in his category. His performance review and bonus depended on it. At the point he met Three Charms, Jeff was trending just above three percent growth and working hard to

---

[3] We've omitted the company's name and changed the brand to "Three Charms" on the advice of counsel (their counsel)...

improve. Placing Three Charms beans on the shelf—in a prominent position—would reduce sales of more expensive beans, slowing Gaines's revenue growth. In the end, it wasn't Jeff's conscience or his concern for the customer that put those beans on the shelf. From a strategy standpoint, he simply knew he needed to introduce the lowest-priced option. So if he had to do it, he'd protect his revenues in the process. Hiding Three Charms in the bottom right solved the problem. **Jeff never shared his concerns with his boss.** When the two of them went through his display plan, Jeff justified the placement of Three Charms Beans through a number of logical arguments. None of them included what he was really thinking.

To Jeff's credit, the Hiding-the-Three-Charms-Beans-On-the-Bottom-Shelf story was one he didn't have to share. In the moment he stood there with his peers, he felt convicted. The Jeff of two years prior had been afraid, selfish, and silent. He assuaged his substantial guilt with a confession to his Core Customer Challenge teammates. At the same time, he intended for everyone to learn from his lack of prior courage. He also vowed to never again put his personal interests before the needs of the customer.

This book is not about Jeff Gaines per se. Time and again when we teach this material, people want to know how to raise arguments in the right way, be more persuasive, or have more fortitude. They inevitably drift in their mind to their own leader—what he or she could do better to elicit conversation. Those things all matter. But they are not what we are addressing in these pages. SAY ANYTHING is at its core a leadership book, but it's not about your leaders, and their virtues or vices, and how you speak to them. It's a leadership book about **YOU** and how you lead your teams. It will cover the obstacles to your people speaking fearlessly. What are the consequences of these muted voices? It will discuss the costs of silence and the benefits of uninhibited communication. It will ask and answer what can you do so your people speak up—anytime and all the time. **SAY ANYTHING** provides research, stories, and, most important, practical steps to leading in a way that brings your people's thoughts and ideas from inside their own heads and out into the open.

Consider Jeff Gaines one last time. Most will empathize with the push and pull of competing interests: customers, strategy, and Jeff's own job performance. In his mid-twenties, trying to launch a long-term career with the company, he had three reasonable options:

1. Reject Three Charms;
2. Put the new brand of beans on the shelf; or
3. Make Three Charms available, but in a place customers probably wouldn't see the beans.

In the world in which many of us reside—the one where people measure their words, hide their thoughts, and speak only when they know it's safe—Jeff settled on the hide-and-seek-the-beans option. Say Anything leadership creates a fourth possibility: Jeff Gaines explains to his leader exactly what he's thinking:

"You know, boss, if I put the Three Charms Beans right in the middle, it will cannibalize my other sales. My revenues will drop below target, and I won't get my bonus. I'll look like I'm failing. But I can't <u>not</u> offer them. They are the lowest price on the market. I want to do what's right for the customer and company, but I'm not going to make four percent if I do that. I don't know what to do. *I need your help."*

We've queried thousands of leaders regarding scenarios similar to Three Charms Beans. Literally *no one* has ever stood up in one of our classrooms and suggested they wouldn't want to hear Jeff's vulnerable admission and request for guidance. The benefits of this type of candor are immediate and self-evident: instead of Jeff placing the product beneath the normal customer's sight line, he uncovers a different solution with his boss.[4] The company benefits. The customer benefits. Jeff does the right thing. Trust ensues, and Jeff opens up a little more confidently the next time he faces a dilemma.

But truth is, outside the safety of a classroom, few conversations like these take place. People hide from their leaders—all the time. We do it. You do it. The people you lead do it. When your people don't speak up, it's not their problem, it's yours. It is the leader's responsibility to create an authentic environment characterized by honesty and trust that

---

[4]We've heard all kinds of creative alternatives from seasoned merchandising executives.

encourages everyone to share their captive thoughts and their original ideas. When you do, the lowly field goal kickers of the world—at the most critical moments—declare: "We shouldn't kick this; it's not the right decision."

Three key **dynamics** stand between your people's thoughts and your ears.

1. The suffocating aura of your own **power**

2. The stinging bite of **past experience**

3. The fear of **judgment and disapproval**

This trio of inhibitors makes candor and openness seemingly unsafe. They are why Jeff Gaines kept his thoughts locked inside his own head and never even considered the words: "I don't know what to do, boss. I need help."

The first step in overcoming—the center of gravity of this book—is to assume positive intent every time someone you lead has the courage to speak up. Nothing will kill Jeff Gaines' option number four more quickly than the way in which you interpret his words (and the resulting look on your face and tone of your response). We make an impassioned yet research-backed case for the power of assuming positive intent, and then provide guideposts for unleashing the voices of those you lead:

1. **Prove It's Safe**: make your appreciation for candid communication explicit, jump into the water first by speaking vulnerably, and, if needed, rope off some small boundaries.

2. **Dignify Every Try**: when your people start to jump in and speak up, honor the slightest (or even most awkward) try. Make a big deal of it and inspire them to continue. And...

3. **Be Genuinely Curious**: don't weigh down good ideas with your anchor, ask Authentic Questions, and encourage the soft-spoken.

In the end, we'll demonstrate what it looks like—this culture where every individual in every corner of the organization knows in her heart and understands with her mind she can voice the most sensitive concern, share every wild idea, and recommend any improvement not only without fear, but with assurance that her leaders will celebrate her tries—both good and bad. We will provide a glimpse of the promised land—and on the way, we will shine a light on all the resulting benefits.

3. IN THE TANK

*Nearly all men can stand adversity,
but if you want to test a man's
character, give him power.*
-Abraham Lincoln

My friend Jamie and I believe we're the two smartest guys in our fantasy football league, but over the course of eighteen years, neither of us has won the WFFL Will Brooks Trophy.[5] We've both failed to mount that glorious piece of hardware on our mantel, going a combined 0-7 in title games. We're just unlucky—really unlucky; two decades worth of unlucky; Priest Holmes breaks his leg a week before the title game unlucky. Jamie now serves as the head of retail banking for of one of the world's most innovative and trusted financial companies, but he still comes up short in fantasy football, every year.

When Jamie isn't losing fantasy football games, he's sending me texts with new ideas. One time around the outset of the millennium the idea was "Fantasy Football Genie"—an algorithm designed to help owners make difficult lineup decisions. He thought we could build it, market it, and sell it to Yahoo! or AOL for millions. I delayed him long enough on the genie thing that he moved to a social

---

[5] Will Brooks was an original league member who infamously drafted Rocket Ismail two years after he retired from the NFL. A move like that gets your name on the trophy.

network where you connect with old friends, share your status, and post pictures.[6] I told him that would never work. Months later he suggested an online college admissions counseling service. Admit Insights —as we would come to call it—began as a simple odds-maker. Prospective college applicants entered their vitals (GPA, SAT, class rank) into a website form, selected five schools they'd like to attend, and a few clicks later received their chances of gaining admission to Yale, Florida, UCLA, Iowa State, Western Oregon, or any mix of several thousand institutions. There were probably a hundred other startups doing the same thing when we set out to launch _www.mychances.com_ (our original name). We slogged through months of brainstorming and multiple iterations of the business plan before landing on the Admit Insights concept. The new website would collect additional info—extra-curricular activities, athletics, honors and awards, grade patterns—and return a comprehensive, eight-page counseling report.[7]

We hired a web hosting company to design and run the site, recruited a few advisors, and purchased ad space in _U.S. News and World Report's_ College Rankings edition. Jamie—a Harvard MBA and electrical engineering major at West Point—developed the proprietary admissions engine in his spare time. I took on the marketing and branding. As part of the efforts, we changed the name and brought in a fresh new logo on the cheap. I even fired off an email to

---

[6] I made this part up to see if you were still paying attention.

[7] "Add an additional year of foreign language," for instance.

Shark Tank, a new television show which provided entrepreneurs an opportunity to pitch their ideas to celebrity investors. The "Sharks," as they were called, doled out real money for equity shares of start-up companies. It was made-for-TV venture capitalism.

Then I bowed out. I was writing a book, starting a different company, and coaching youth basketball. Admit Insights proved a better idea than Fantasy Football Genie, but it wasn't going to feed my family.

Nine months later my phone rang. A young-sounding guy squealed excitedly, "Hey! This is Brad from *Shark Tank*. Is this Doug?" I cocked my head sideways like a puzzled golden retriever and looked out the window of our den. Maybe two seconds passed. I replied: "Um, yeah, this is Doug." Brad went on to explain they really loved our story—especially the West Point angle—and wondered if we were still interested in the show. It had seriously been more than *nine months* since I applied. Children who hadn't even been conceived when I sent the email had now been born. I figured ABC canceled the series long ago.

Not the case—*Shark Tank* was coming back for a second season with Jeff Foxworthy, Mark Cuban, and Admit Insights. Jamie and I had a solid business idea, a promising management team, and an intriguing backstory (Admit Insights had since brought in Kevin Vaughn, a star running back and Jamie's study partner at West Point). Brad, the *Shark Tank* guy, had one concern: we were boring. We didn't have the quirky appeal of the Man Candles founder or the sentimental angle of two young kids who created

Flipoutz arm bands. We definitely weren't Wake n' Bacon—the alarm clock whose special trick was to provide two warm, crispy strips of breakfast meat as you awoke. Admit Insights was just three West Point classmates with a fairly legit business model.

Brad beat us up on the phone for weeks. We had to speak with more passion, create an emotional angle, and give the Sharks (and the television audience) something they could root for. Going behind the curtain of a reality TV show proved enlightening. Brad was one of many co-producers attempting to sell his prized prospects to Mark Burnett.[8] We never met Burnett, who had a bit of a Wizard of Oz thing going, but we spent hours with Brad. When we finally got to Hollywood, Brad fed us more advice: the three of us were too stoic. He wanted us to crank up the demonstrative. Almost like it was final exams at West Point again, we crashed for the test, working our lines, our hand gestures, and our transitions until our ninety-second opening was seamless. We drove to the studio in a van with the Flipoutz family and two attractive women selling a fitness regimen. We then sat behind a forest of spotlights in an arrangement of folding chairs, anticipating the final tryout. We waited for hours. We were fortunate, however. Of the forty-plus entrepreneurs the show had flown to Hollywood, only three-quarters even auditioned in front of Burnett's advisors. We got our shot late in the day, and cleared the final hurdle. Sort of.

---

[8] The creator of *Survivor*, *The Apprentice*, *The Voice*, and really American reality television. By the way—he's British.

The next morning, Man Candles, Bacon, and Flipoutz all received calls to the studio. We stood by again. Brad told us we might be picked, but we might not. Then sometime after lunch, a young woman knocked on our hotel room door, gave us some per diem money, and escorted us to a van. A driver shuttled us back to the studio. We waited some more in a room that smelled like a canvas tent that never fully dried before being stored in a dusty attic for months. Kevin, Jamie, and I were the last team to go into the *Shark Tank* that day. As I remember it, we were the final act to audition for the entire second season of the show. In our dressing room—before we got to the canvas-smelling holding cell—Brad came in and told us we could speak to an on-site psychologist after we finished up presenting to the Sharks. I remember my exact thoughts:

A psychologist? That's so southern-California. Only in Hollywood would they offer you the services of a psychologist. It's a business pitch, not a firefight in Afghanistan.

A few hours later, we straightened our belts, tucked in our shirts, and walked through the double doors and down the hall into the *Shark Tank*. We took our mark exactly where they'd told us. Standing just twenty feet from Mark Cuban made my heart pound. The 6'3" Dallas Mavericks owner was intimidating, even seated in his plush leather chair. I launched the pitch: "My son John," I pled with a quivering lip and clenched fist, "I love him with all my heart. He's always dreamed of attending the University of

Washington…" The plea felt a little overdone, but Brad had insisted. We had to connect emotionally. As the pitch transitioned to Kevin, my mind wandered to the substantial amount of makeup on the Sharks' faces. Jamie finished up his portion of the Admit Insights' story by asking for an investment.

I was surprisingly nervous. I'd spoken to crowds of thousands at that point in life—loved public speaking in fact. But this was different. It felt risky in a personal way. As each moment passed, we waited for one of the five discriminating figureheads to say "I'm out." Robert Herjavec mentioned the college admissions gauntlet his own children navigated and praised the merits of our idea, but he was "out." As soon as Robert bailed, my body started pumping sweat out all my pores. It was as if my palms were crying. *Wait*, I thought to myself, *let me rewind and say that last thing differently.*

At some point, Daymond John looked right at me and asked: "Doug, take a look at all the Sharks. What's different about me?"

Crud. Why was the only non-Caucasian Shark asking me this? Did I look like a racist? Had I said something wrong earlier in the conversation? Was this a test of my candor?

This guy founded FUBU.[9] He could crush me with his pinky. Mark Cuban smirked a bit as I considered Daymond's question. I'd seen people go down in flames saying the wrong thing in life. As a cadet at West Point, I apparently chose incorrect words during a Bible study. An officer made fun of me. I never went

---

[9] "For Us By Us"

back. This moment might be on national television. Millions of people were going to hear my answer. Daymond John wants me to tell him how he's different from the other Sharks? The only thing positive about this situation was how quickly my mind was proving it could race. "Come on, Doug..." Daymond scolded.

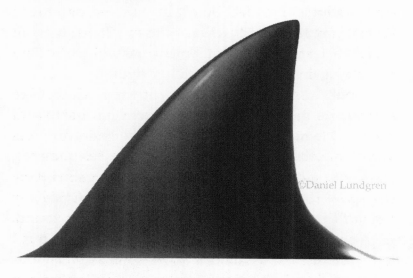

©Daniel Lundgren

"Well, um, you're African-American?" *Oh noooooo. Why didn't I say he was bald? But Kevin O'Leary's bald too. Are we screwed?*

Remember in *A Christmas Story* when Ralphie says the f-word? His dad is changing a tire, and all of a sudden a hubcap full of lug nuts goes flying through the air? Young Ralphie fires off a visceral utterance. "Fu......But I didn't say 'fudge.'"

Well, at least I'd called Daymond "African-American." I don't think the guy who founded a clothing label as edgy as FUBU would appreciate me phrasing it: "You're different than the others because you're a brother?"

"No, that's not right," Daymond John retorted. "The difference between these other Sharks and me is I'm smart. **I'm out.**"

I looked to Barbara Corcoran for some relief—almost entirely because she was a woman. She could smile and make me feel better. I was standing next to Kevin Vaughn, clearly a black man. "I have black friends," I wanted to tell Daymond while nodding toward Kevin subtly.

Jamie and Kevin picked up my slack. We eventually secured a contingency-filled deal with Kevin O'Leary.[10] My mind clogged reviewing the verbal diarrhea I'd spewed over those ten minutes. **I'd never felt so powerless, judged, or scared of the consequences of my words.** Every syllable my tongue, lips, and vocal chords mustered into a sound, felt horrifying. I didn't enlist the psychologist, but I left southern California understanding why she was at-the-ready. We ate dinner the evening following our moment in the tank next to a guy who invented tiny nostril covers. He'd pitched them as a way to keep people healthy on airplanes and in other airborne-hazard-filled environments. Admit Insights registered as an afterthought in my own life. It wasn't even important enough for me to claim it as a hobby. The nostril-cover guy had invested all his emotions and financial resources into his idea—only to face the power and judgment of the Sharks. He went in there (like all of us have been) scarred by people who had

---

[10] Known on the show as "Mr. Wonderful."

said "No," laughed at him, or told him it would never work. I admired his fortitude and courage.

A few months later, our deal fell through in the Boston-based offices of McGraw-Hill. We never heard from Kevin O'Leary again. Just three weeks before *Shark Tank* launched its second season, a producer called me on the phone to apologize. They would not be airing our segment. He didn't tell us we were boring. He didn't blame it on my awareness of Daymond John's race. He just told us they didn't have the airtime—hadn't been contracted for enough episodes—to show our piece. My heart registered a combination of disappointment and relief. I didn't want millions of people watching my meltdown.

The *Shark Tank* experience was oddly educational. I learned in those moments how followers must feel when we—leaders who hold the power—judge their words, toss out sarcasm and disapproval, or even just roll our eyes. Members of our teams spend their lives learning how horrifying it can be to speak up, face rejection, or try to answer a question in the right way.

An ABC reality television show, staged on an artificial set, brought me to my knees. I had only a few minutes to make my words count, and the pressure proved surprisingly intense. Power, past experience, and fear of judgment and disapproval—these are the characteristics that turn it into the *Shark Tank*.

If a guy with nothing much to lose, normally bold and verbose, pitching an idea he didn't really care about, to people he didn't even know, in a setting he'd volunteered to enter, needed a psychologist and a shower at the end of twenty minutes, then imagine what's going on in the hearts and minds of your own people. Are power, past experience, and fear of judgment getting in their way and dampening suggestions, ideas, and warnings from which your organization could immeasurably benefit?

As leaders, how do we overcome? How do we instill fearlessness, optimism, and candor into those we lead? We'll get there, but first we must understand the things that hold our people back...

THE DYNAMICS

4. SUFFOCATING POWER

Personalities change when the President is present, and frequently even strong men make recommendations on the basis of what they believe the President wishes to hear.

—Robert F. Kennedy, Thirteen Days

The sun had just peeked over an eastern hill on a fall morning in 1992 when Eddie Sullivan pulled his rusty-red Ford truck into the carport on Bob Guion's homestead. Eddie served as Guion's handyman, and he liked to start his work early to avoid the heat. This particular day, Sullivan was scheduled to tear down an eighty-year-old barn.

A few hours into the demolition, Eddie realized he'd left his crowbar back at his truck. It was a several-hundred yard walk, but he needed the tool. When he reached the vehicle—around ten a.m.—the crowbar was gone. "I looked all around," remembered Eddie, "and that's when I saw Mr. Guion lying in the grass through the breezeway." Sullivan glanced briefly at Bob Guion's bloody, contorted body and dashed up the weathered staircase in a panic to pound on the door. "Call an ambulance," Eddie yelled at Marion Guion, Bob's wife. The police report suggested Robert L. Guion—owner of a local Lincoln dealership—had been assaulted and struck on the left brow as he exited his house for his regular 7 a.m. golf game. Lieutenant Mark Moody, lead investigator, named three primary suspects: Mickey Malone, a parts supplier to Guion's car dealership; Billy Prentice, the yardman; and Eddie Sullivan, the handyman who first discovered Guion's body.

Lt. Moody's focus quickly turned to Malone, whose motive seemed strongest (albeit still questionable). Just a week before the murder, Malone received a handwritten note from Guion voicing displeasure with their business interactions:

> I am very upset about the substandard parts I have been receiving from you...I will have to notify my customers and other dealers about the quality of MM auto parts.

Harsh words, but would the 1992 equivalent of a one-star Yelp rating really be an impetus for murder? Malone admitted he'd been headed to Guion's property that Saturday, ready to confront Bob about the letter. But he'd thought better of it, u-turned on Crestview Highway, and stopped to get some coffee before arriving at the golf course at 7 a.m.

The second suspect, Billy Prentice, had a gambling problem and often approached "Mr. Bob" to borrow money. He'd done so as recently as the afternoon before Guion's death. But this dependence on his boss seemed almost a disincentive to kill him. Absent motive, Prentice proved a dubious suspect—until Lieutenant Moody discovered he had lied in his initial statement, and his fingerprints had been found on the missing crowbar. Confronted with these facts, Prentice reversed course and admitted to being on the property, but said he'd discovered Guion dead at the base of the stairs and fled in fear. He had no idea how his fingerprints ended up on the crowbar or how it ended up in the bushes.

The final suspect, Eddie Sullivan, pointed a limp finger at Prentice, suggesting he'd heard a "car with a loud muffler" speeding away at about seven a.m. The noise was tough to make out from the barn, but he was pretty sure it was Billy. The sound of an accelerating car didn't amount to a murder conviction, but the lying, fingerprints, and gambling problem all constituted a growing pile of circumstantial evidence. Moody just couldn't imagine what Billy Prentice's motive would have been.

Sullivan might have had motive. His daughter worked as the bookkeeper at Bob Guion's dealership until quitting a few weeks before the murder. Eddie claimed he didn't know why his daughter left, but testimony from employees at the dealership revealed her resignation followed a heated argument with Guion. Body language and subtleties in one of the witness interviews even hinted at a possible affair.

But that was it: three suspects, a bunch of circumstantial evidence, and nowhere else to turn. DNA evidence, first used to convict Florida rapist Tommie Lee Andrews in 1987, was still considered a novelty in most venues as late as the mid-1990s. Whoever killed Bob Guion—whether Mickey Malone,

Bobby Prentice, Eddie Sullivan, or someone else—was going to get away with it.

So what if we asked you to take your best guess? Based on three pages summarizing the murder of Bob Guion, who would you choose: Mickey, Billy, or Eddie? With what amount of certainty would you cast your vote? It wouldn't be "beyond a reasonable doubt," but how about "more likely than not?"

Let's take it a step further. You've been designated the leader of a small group, charged with poring over the maps, notes, and interviews collected at the time of the killing. Justice—and a widow's peace of mind —depend on your team's ability to unlock the mystery of this cold case. And although you don't know it, among the stack of notes and interviews are pieces of information which will help you identify, unequivocally, the person who struck Bob Guion with Eddie's crowbar and sent him down the rickety staircase to his death.

One member of your group holds the transcript of an interview with Millie Smith from Ray's Café. Her statement clears Mickey Malone. She corroborates that he was drinking coffee at Ray's from 6:30 a.m. to 6:45 a.m. Another team member knows Billy does, in fact, recall touching the crowbar, but only to move it so he could get the lawnmower out of the covered parking area. This person also holds a statement from Dave Daniels, owner of a Quick Stop just down the street from Guion's house. Daniels found Guion's wallet around 7 a.m. Someone threw it toward the dumpster behind the store and sped away. Whoever ditched the wallet was in a car that "ran real quiet."

Last are statements from Marion Guion. Not everyone you lead in this effort to solve the murder knows Mrs. Guion looked out her window at 6:40 a.m. All she saw in the covered parking area was Bob's pickup. She also informed police that Eddie has a hearing aid, but never wears it when he works.

Mickey Malone didn't kill Bob Guion. He has an alibi. Billy Prentice had no motive, was completely forthright (after he wasn't), and it wasn't his loud truck which dumped the wallet next to Dave Daniels's dumpster. So the good news for your team? You can pinpoint Eddie Sullivan as the killer. He lied when he claimed to have heard Billy's truck.[11] He had motive and opportunity, and when Marion looked out the window at 6:40 a.m., Eddie's truck was gone.

The bad news? Research—thorough and compelling research—demonstrates that leaders will get in the way of solving problems such as *The Case of the Fallen Businessman*.[12] The mystery of Robert Guion is a seminal study in group communication constructed by Gary Stasser of Miami (Ohio) University. Stasser discovered open communication is difficult in small groups. People tend to share common knowledge, but are afraid of looking foolish by voicing things only

---

[11]He couldn't have identified the low-quality muffler from several hundred yards without the benefit of his hearing aid.

[12] A fictional story, fortunately.

they know. Group members question themselves: *if it's relevant, why has no one else brought this up?*

I remember experiencing this personally in eighth grade.[13] My best friend Eddie and I were in the back of a car on the way to a beach party. Meggan Young's mom seemed a bit lost, and we started to wander, slowing down at every street sign. Eddie and I had been entertaining the group with our rendition of a Sesame Street classic. I sang "I've got two eyes," in my pre-pubescent voice, and Eddie followed with "one…two," in a much deeper octave. Cute girls laughed. Eddie and I kept singing.

Out the right window, I spotted a sign:

Party this way —>

No one else seemed to have seen it. I knew something the others didn't. But I talked myself out of sharing it (at least right away).

---

[13] If you missed the author's note—all the first person stories in **SAY ANYTHING** belong to Doug. He's older and has done a lot more stupid stuff than Matt. We thought it would be easier.

What if I was wrong?

What if Mrs. Young doesn't like me telling her which way to go?

What if the girls think I'm rude?

Maybe it was a different party?

We drove around for another five minutes until I finally spoke up: "I think I saw a sign back there?" Everyone groaned. Why didn't you tell us earlier? My reasons for not sharing my knowledge were mostly lame, but they still kept me quiet in a non-threatening situation. I built up obstacles inside my own psyche.

The bad news gets worse—much worse—when formal leaders who feel powerful enter the fray. Power wreaks all kinds of havoc:

It elevates a leader's tendency to objectify others (you see others as means to your ends).

It renders a leader tone-deaf to others' perspectives.

It leaves a leader more prone to stereotype.

It depletes a leader's willingness to listen.

Not a good list.

Power is so powerful, in fact, when Leigh Plunkett Tost, Francesca Gino, and Richard Larrick[14] put power-primed leaders in charge of a team tasked to solve the Bob Guion murder, the leaders failed miserably. Groups with formal leaders who had been primed to feel powerful tagged Eddie Sullivan as the culprit only *twenty-five percent* of the time. On the other hand, when there was no leader at all, groups solved the mystery *fifty-nine percent* of the time. Astounding difference. Put more plainly: leaders (you and I) suck at this stuff. When placed in charge, we puff our chests, run our mouths, and get in the way.

"Powerful" leader ⟶ 25% success

No leader at all ⟶ 59% success

In the murder mystery experiment, random participants wore nametags designating them as leaders. That's it. A nametag and an induced feeling of power (via pre-experiment reflection) resulted in communication-stifling dominance. Tost, Gino, and Larrick discovered *leaders who feel powerful talk too much*. We dominate group discussions, shutting

---

[14] Of Michigan, Harvard, and Duke respectively.

others down and devaluing them personally. A few years ago, a participant in one of our programs made a courageous admission to the group: "I constantly have discussions with my team where I'm just trying to lead them to my idea and get their buy-in." Hesitantly, but almost therapeutically, she continued, "I've been promoted all along because people said I had great ideas. I guess it's hard to stop being the one with the ideas and instead someone who gets others to share theirs." It's not evil leaders who do this—talk too much, focus on themselves, and devalue the input of those they lead. We all do it to some extent. It's a human tendency. As a result, rather than sharing information that might help solve a problem, spark innovation, or avoid crises, group members say little.

Matt teaches executive communications at a small college in south-central Washington. His sections are full of adult learners—men and women putting in tough hours during the day, running home to whip up dinner for their family, and then heading across town to take one more step toward a bachelor's degree. This Say Anything concept had been top-of-mind for Matt as we researched, discussed, outlined, and revised. One evening, he posed a question to students:

"What would you like to say to your boss?"

A chorus of emotionally charged answers flew at Matt's head. Some of the professionals—having lost the capacity to care—threw out things that made Matt and the entire rest of the class laugh. None of the answers seemed unreasonable. They certainly weren't mean-spirited or personal remarks. When he probed as to why his students left all these things unsaid, one gentleman boldly professed, "You're asking me to choose between my ego and my livelihood!" The man genuinely feared if he voiced his true sentiments, his boss would hold it against him until eventually showing him the door. What was the super-scary statement this guy kept locked away in secret? "I'd like to explain that when he procrastinates, it makes my job more difficult."

He deeply wanted his boss to know this, yet the idea of actually bringing it up, in his eyes, would get him fired. This wasn't someone looking upward in the pecking order of an inner-city gang or distributing cocaine for a drug cartel in Central America. He toiled daily as a mid-level leader employed at a publicly traded corporation headquartered in San Francisco. But where powerful sharks swim, people refuse to become the bait. Professor Adam Grant of Wharton calls these power-filled leaders takers: [15]

> Although group members perceive takers as highly effective leaders, takers actually undermine group performance. Speaking dominantly convinces group members that takers are powerful, but it stifles information sharing, preventing members from communicating good ideas.

---

[15]People who strive to get as much as possible from others.

Grant concocted an experiment much more simple than solving a murder to demonstrate the effect. His colleagues and he brought teams together to fold t-shirts. In half of the groups, leaders were instructed to speak with force and direct the group. Prior to the experiment, they even spent some time reading about the merits of extroverts. The other half did not read up on extroverts and received guidance to temper their input and lead quietly: "There are others in the group who have contributions to make," the researchers reminded. On the teams with quiet leaders who remained supportive and welcomed suggestions, output came in twenty-two percent higher. Grant points out some may see such receptive, deferent leaders as weak. **If looking good is your goal, we recommend talking a lot. However, if performance is your objective, we recommend you lead in a way that encourages others to speak up.**

These murder scenarios and t-shirt folding sessions were experiments. Imagine the implications when your power exists legitimately and comes in the form of rank, title, charisma, or expertise…In his book *Outliers*, Malcolm Gladwell cites a memorable fact from the annals of the airline industry:

> Captains and first officers split the flying duties equally. But historically, crashes have been far more likely to happen when the captain is in the "flying seat." At first that seems to make no sense, since the captain is almost always the pilot with the most experience.

But when explained, it makes all the sense in the world. Captains will *command* while first officers will *suggest* or *hint*. It's the difference between *"turn thirty degrees right"* and *"I think it might be wise to turn left or right if you get the chance."*

"Planes are safer when the least experienced pilot is flying," Gladwell explains, "because it means the second pilot isn't going to be afraid to speak up."

The *USS Greeneville* is a Los Angeles-class, fast-attack, nuclear submarine armed with Tomahawk missiles. Commissioned in 1994, it measures 363 feet and weighs 7,177 tons. On February 9, 2001, the sub departed for standard maneuvers off the shores of Oahu as part of a "distinguished visitor cruise"—a program intended to provide influential civilians insight into navy operations. When the Greeneville executed an emergency main ballast tank blow nine miles shy of port, a businessman occupied the helmsman chair and a sports reporter operated the valve levers. Experienced crew members supervised these guests closely while Captain Scott Waddle delivered instructions. "Emergency" main ballast blow is somewhat of a misnomer. The procedure is pretty standard. The crew brings the submarine to periscope depth (60 feet), sweeps the area above water for other ships, and then blows out its ballast tanks to surface rapidly. Emerging from the water, a Los Angeles class submarine looks like a giant torpedo. On this day, the *Greeneville* failed to complete its rapid surface. According to the National Transportation Safety Board's official report:

The guests quoted the commander as saying, "What the hell was that?" After the submarine slowed and the periscope could be raised, the CO looked into the periscope and announced that the submarine had struck another ship.

The *Ehime Maru*—a five-hundred-ton Japanese fishing boat—never had a chance. A football-field-sized projectile surfaced rapidly at 1:43 p.m., Hawaiian standard time. The *Greeneville* sliced the *Ehime Maru* in half, sinking it in minutes and killing nine crew members. The presence of guests complicated operations that day. Captain Waddle, the commander, and his executive officer had spent an hour of the afternoon in the captain's cabin signing photographs. Some reports suggested Waddle rushed the surfacing procedures because certain guests were going to be late for a meeting. The distractions undoubtedly diminished the CO's situational awareness. But in the end, the NTSB cited communication issues—the failure of the crew to Say Anything—as the cause of the accident. Or, we might put it another way: the failure of leadership to cultivate a climate where people could speak candidly.

The National Transportation Safety Board determines that the probable cause of the collision of the USS Greeneville with the Japanese fisheries training vessel Ehime Maru was the inadequate interaction and communication among senior members of the combat systems team (the commanding officer, the officer of the deck, the fire control technician, and the sonar supervisor), which resulted in the failure to perform adequate contact analysis and adhere to proper procedures for moving to periscope depth; and the commanding officer's decision to order an emergency surfacing maneuver.

It's difficult to speak truth to power.

Scott Waddle graduated at the top of his class from the U.S. Naval Academy. He was a rising star with an impeccable performance record, chosen from among hundreds of qualified officers to command the *USS Greeneville*. Some say there's no more intoxicating position than captain of a ship at sea. But on that day, Waddle rushed procedure at the very least. The sonar picture was murky. The commander's own periscope check (which no one wanted to question) seemed perfunctory. Critics claim Waddle never ascended high enough with the periscope to get a true picture of traffic on the surface. For crew members, speaking up in the moment would have meant correcting the commanding officer in front of sixteen distinguished visitors. Waddle was high-ranking, competent, and respected. This wasn't a case of a tyrant scowling at his subjects. This was typical interaction among leader and followers. Only the result was extraordinary.

Excuse me, sir, but I don't think we should surface.

I made the decision. Just do your job. Lieutenant.

"The moment a leader allows himself to become the primary reality people worry about, rather than reality being the primary reality," observes Jim Collins. "you have a recipe for mediocrity or worse." Suddenly ending the lives of nine innocent Japanese fishermen = worse.

We're not suggesting people Say Anything to their daughter's coach, their neighbor, their flight attendant, or their Facebook friends. We are all for tact, respect, and emotional intelligence. But when you have the upper hand in the relationship—when you are the leader—your people should be able to Say Anything to you. They won't—unless you work tirelessly to mitigate the unintended effects of your power. And quite frankly, if you feel compelled to *actively* remind others of your position, you'll never have a chance to hear what the people you lead truly want to say. It's really a combination of ego and power you must set aside to reap the benefits of so many voices. When those you lead Say Anything, it will be inevitably messy, sticky, and sometimes painful. They'll do it imperfectly (to be certain). You'll want to fire back with your own words. The finesse, skill, and timing can come later—once you've established an environment where your own power is not the ten-pound gavel and the ultimate trump card.

5. ONCE BITTEN

I heard a great story recently, I love telling it, of a little girl who was in a drawing lesson. She was 6, and she was at the back, drawing, and the teacher said this little girl hardly paid attention, and in this drawing lesson she did. The teacher was fascinated and she went over to her and she said, "What are you drawing?" And the girl said, "I'm drawing a picture of God." And the teacher said, "But nobody knows what God looks like." And the girl said, "They will in a minute."
– Sir Ken Robinson

Sir Ken Robinson's brilliant musing on *How Schools Kill Creativity* is the most watched TED talk of all time.[16] Nearly thirty million people have tuned in since he delivered it in 2006. Sir Ken makes an intriguing observation: "Kids will take a chance. If they don't know, they'll have a go. Am I right? They're not afraid of being wrong." In the TED talk, Robinson speaks primarily about creativity, suggesting corporations stigmatize mistakes. "If you're not prepared to be wrong," he argues, "you'll never come up with anything original...we are educating people out of their creative capacities."

A confident kindergartner might make a better officer of the deck than a culturally conditioned Navy lieutenant. The hand would

---

[16] www.ted.com

shoot up, lips would purse, and Samantha would let the captain have it: "We need to go higher with the periscope." But kids become adults—adults with inhibitions, hesitations, and fears. As we grow up, or really as our hands get smacked time and again, we unlearn to say what we think.

There's a psychological concept called "flashbulb memory." Never mind that we are only a few years away from no one remembering what a flashbulb was; the concept explains the pictures we see in our heads of certain moments in time. Some of them we share: where you were when you heard JFK had been shot, saw the Challenger explode, or were told two planes flew into the World Trade Center buildings. Others are ours alone: a first kiss, the birth of a child, or the death of a parent. In these moments such powerful emotions stir within us that our brain "takes a picture" and stores it in long-term memory. Ten years later we can see what we were wearing, who sat next to us, and what time was on the clock.

The year before I enrolled in kindergarten, I attended Highland Christian School in Bellevue, Washington. The school's mascot is a friendly looking teddy bear wearing a yellow sweater and waving a red flag that says "HCS." My recollections aren't as warm and fuzzy. I have flashbulb memory of a moment in Mrs. Patterson's pre-school class at Highland Christian. Our group of twenty had gathered together in front of a small, wooden stage. I sat in the back of the pack, legs crisscrossed, wearing a green and white striped turtleneck and jeans. We were talking about traffic lights. Somebody told Mrs. Patterson you "go on red and stop on green." Being a judgmental, know-it-all five-year-old, I shot my hand up in the air to correct my moronic classmate. And I didn't wait for Mrs. Patterson to call on me. "No!" I exclaimed with indignation, "You go on green and you stop on red." The entire movie in my mind is only four or five seconds long, but what happened next has stayed with me my entire life.

The soundtrack, more than the video, is etched into my brain: "Douglas," Mrs. Patterson scolded back, "stop lying!" The next thing I can remember, my brother (nine years older) and I were sitting in my room. My NFL-themed bedspread had a large, checkered pattern. Rob pointed to an intersection of lines and explained Mrs. Patterson probably meant, when looking at the light kitty-corner from where you're standing, you go when it's red and you stop when it's green. I still didn't get why you wouldn't just look at your own light, and I knew for sure I wasn't a liar. I knew something else: I wasn't raising my hand at Highland Christian anymore.

That was nearly forty years ago. I'm over it (almost), but it left a mark. I can still hear Mrs. Patterson's dominant tone, and I can see vividly the shadows of her angry face and the towering height of her dark brown, beehive hairdo. The people you lead have likely never encountered my preschool teacher, but someone, somewhere, robbed them of their eagerness to contribute. I told the Mrs. Patterson story during a session with mid-level leaders at a large company. When done, I asked if anyone had examples of "Say Anything" stories. A gentleman in the front row raised his hand and sheepishly began to share. He'd spent his entire career in finance, but one day his boss assigned him a complex marketing project. She told him to attack the task, but knew it was not his area of expertise. "If you get stuck," she consoled, "if you need any help, just let me know. Worst case—if it's simply beyond your scope—we can assign it to someone else. But I'd like you to try."

The executive battled the marketing project for two weeks, but he floundered. "I just didn't have the ability to do it well. I'm a finance guy and it was a marketing project—and an important one. So I went to my boss, and I told her I needed help—told her I thought it would be better if someone else took the lead. She paused for a moment, then looked right at me and declared in a harsh tone: 'You never say that around here. Never tell people you can't do something. Say that around here, and it'll get around. Your career will be over.'"

You can't make this stuff up.

"I learned," he explained, "never to speak up around here again. I just keep my mouth shut." From that moment forward, what was best for the organization became subordinate to his fears of asking for help or admitting he needed assistance. His own boss—the leader charged with answering his questions, providing him guidance, and developing his talents—instead became a predator lurking in the tall grass.

One of my West Point classmates commanded an infantry battalion during the height of the War on Terror. Since his days as a cadet, this guy had been an impressively intense, exceedingly honest, and unflinchingly outspoken leader. Shortly following a taxing, twelve-month deployment to Iraq (their fourth since 9-11), planners called upon the unit to deploy with extremely limited notice to perform a mission they had never trained for. The lieutenant colonel surveyed the readiness of his soldiers, their tactical acumen for this task, and their equipment, and told his commander: "I don't think we are prepared. Of course we will go, but you know, sir, there are much better options for this mission."

Those are painful (almost humiliating) statements for an army officer to verbalize. Having graduated from an institution where he spent the first six weeks of his existence saying: "Yes, sir," "No, ma'am," or "No excuse, sir," Doug's friend could hardly believe the words coming out of his own mouth. This was a professional who had been promoted early to major,[17] lauded at every stop in his career, and revered by his soldiers. He wasn't trying to avoid more time away from home (although that would have been understandable). He spoke up in this instance because his team had experienced personnel turnover and casualties. There were still-healing psychological wounds. The families were exhausted, and the soldiers were being asked to perform a mission they had never trained for in a place his unit had never deployed to. The commander stated candidly the unit wasn't the best option and wouldn't be ready in the time allocated.

The brigade commander went to the division commander and discussed the situation. He then

---

[17] Placing him in the top seven percent of his peers.

returned and praised his direct report for an uncommon display of honesty—a countercultural testament to his love and concern for those he led.

Actually, that is **not** at all what he did. He came back from division, and berated the lieutenant colonel for "frankly not being as excited" as the brigade commander thought he should be. In the end, the officer took the battalion to Afghanistan. As he said later on, "No way was I going to let another commander take my boys to this fight, especially with so little notification and preparation." For obvious reasons, Doug's classmate asked that we not use his name. He's still hoping he might make colonel, and continues to face the repercussions of the disapproval and judgment. *We're ready, sir. Absolutely. One hundred percent. Would you like to see how well I salute?*

"We're not ready."

"I'm sorry."

"I don't understand where we're headed."

"I need help."

"The timing isn't right."

"That's not a good idea."

*"I have an idea
that's a little out there."*

"This isn't going well."

"We should check one more time."

*"I think we'd do better
if you backed off."*

"We could have done better."

These and many others are the things people learn not to say. Culture teaches what's safe and acceptable, and what's punished or rewarded.

VitalSmarts, in conjunction with a couple nursing organizations, conducted two in-depth studies of communication in healthcare.[18] Among other things, the studies pointed out that fifty-eight percent of surveyed nurses admitted "they had been in situations where it was either unsafe to speak up or they were unable to get someone to listen."

Sometimes the situations are tricky, such as an experienced doctor whose incompetence threatens a patient. We can all empathize with the difficulty of voicing your thoughts in such a scenario. But others are simple:

---

[18] VitalSmarts is a leadership consultancy. AACN and AORN were the nursing organizations. The studies were *Silence Kills* in 2005 and *The Silent Treatment* in 2010.

Each year 1 in 20 patients at hospitals will be given a wrong medication, 3.5 million will get an infection from someone who didn't wash his or her hands or take other appropriate precautions, and 195,000 will die because of mistakes made while they're in the hospital.

The combined capacity of Yankee Stadium, the Louisiana Superdome, and CenturyLink Field in Seattle would fall fifteen hundred seats short of accommodating those who die in our medical facilities *each year* due to errors potentially preventable by fostering environments where everyone speaks freely—where people can say plainly, "You forgot to wash your hands."

Instead, nurses learn to keep quiet. *Silence Kills* cites research on organizational communication and concludes, "Solving undiscussables will require deeper changes to cultural practices, social norms, and personal skills." We don't disagree that culture creates much of the problem—culture shows new members what to say and what not to say. It's absolutely something leaders must overcome in the quest to liberate every voice. But as the leader(s), you shape culture. Leaders control what happens in their lane through their words, actions, and most importantly their mindset (as we will discover later). Consider how this nurse's chilling account will shape her and her peers. She had a concern for a patient's safety, so she contacted the doctor on call:

The surgeon was at a dinner party...and was very vocal about how much trouble I would be in if he had to come back to the hospital for no reason. He came back and took the patient into surgery. The leg had occluded. I was never so nervous about the outcome, and was so relieved to have been correct.

This nurse was "relieved" she was correct—so she wouldn't receive a lashing from the surgeon—even though it meant the patient was in trouble.

VitalSmarts trains low-power healthcare workers in skills necessary for speaking up. At the conclusion of their report, the authors portray characteristics of exceptional nurses—those who speak up fearlessly: "They begin by explaining their positive intent [and] use facts and data as much as possible..." VitalSmarts re-educates people. They teach them how to do what they weren't afraid to do in kindergarten. It's a necessary skill in cultures of silence. But what if leaders disposed of the nonsense, set aside ego, valued everyone's perspective, and intentionally elicited input.[19] Wouldn't that be so much easier? And smarter? And less exhausting? And more efficient? And just plain better?

> *"You better not interrupt
> my dinner party."*

Seriously?

---

[19] Another major stumbling block is leader insecurity. It's a book in and of itself: self-awareness and self-management. SAY ANYTHING is helpful only to those who admit they are part of the problem (or the entire problem).

Laura Lothrop had an idea. She had lots of them. After earning her degree in education and teaching for a brief period, she spent a decade-plus raising five kids while helping her husband build a wildly successful business. There were early days when she held a Motorola in one hand (dispatching drivers to various locations) and a newborn in the other. The living room was her office, the couch was her chair, and a Playskool table was her desk. But in 2004, it all unraveled. Laura experienced a bitter divorce. Seemingly a hundred legal battles later, she'd lost her house, her car, and her half of the company. She prepared food at a restaurant in a casino, studied to earn a financial planning certificate, and shuttled kids to soccer, school, and their father's house.

Lothrop struck a break in the fall of 2011. She'd submitted an online application to work at a local retailer. Hole-in-ones during Saturday golf games, winning PowerBall tickets, and picking the right stocks are all things with better odds than landing an interview via Monster.com, but Laura received a call. The regional manager directed stores to seek out and hire one or two "external" assistant managers. Laura's degree and business experience impressed the store manager, and he brought her in. A few weeks later, Lothrop started a new job. Although she had just turned fifty, she looked ahead with anticipation. The company offered ample growth potential, and she felt confident she could contribute immediately. She earned the highest marks at a six-week training course for new managers and encouragement she would ascend rapidly based on her leadership acumen and professionalism.

When she returned from training, one of Laura's initial responsibilities involved resurrecting a poorly performing outdoor living section. She worked tirelessly to recruit the right people, implement proper procedures, and meet her supervisor's expectations. It was a steep climb. Most of her peers didn't appreciate an external hire coming into the mix. Laura's boss, Elaine, seemed to like it even less. She was downright nasty.

But knowing this was her chance, Laura Lothrop soldiered on. She spent ample time with shoppers, listening to their issues and concerns. One developing theme involved the re-potting of plants. A number of customers asked about transplanting, worried they'd kill their vegetation in the process and thus hesitant to attempt the process. Their fears prevented them from purchasing containers. Laura saw an opportunity. Her memory returned her to a horticulture elective she'd taken in high school. She recalled plants should be moved to a pot two inches larger in diameter every six months. The store could set up a small station, quickly teaching customers how to transplant safely while also informing them of the two-inch rule. The three-minute education would provide a valuable service and sell more merchandise.

Laura took the idea to her boss. She hoped this would be the first of many ways she could add value through creativity and innovation. She was more excited to share her idea than she'd been in a long time. What she lacked in understanding of company operations and retail practices, she would compensate for through a fresh perspective and new thinking—which is exactly why the company hired her externally in the first place. But Laura *learned* otherwise. "Just do your job," her manager told her. "Stop with the silly ideas and take care of the day-to-day." She texted her brother that afternoon, hoping he could console her. "I guess I'll just bide my time. Not going to make any more suggestions until I have my own store." That time never came. Laura left the company nine months later.[20]

If Laura Lothrop is your next employee, you're facing an uphill battle earning her trust. It will be awhile before she vocalizes an area needing improvement, raises her hand with a new idea, or admits she doesn't quite understand. Her last boss—and the culture of her last organization—taught her to put her head down and just do her job. Millions of creative, intelligent, and eager people are living out their lives in the same way all around us. And inside every one of them is a spirited kindergartner just dying to raise his or her hand and change your organization for the better.

---

[20] We later shared this story with a vice president at the company. Before we could deliver the punchline (that Laura had been shut down), the executive proclaimed: "That's a great idea. We could get the vendors to pay for the station and sell more merchandise."

6. FEAR OF JUDGMENT

*In our organization there's a mold,
and if you don't fit the mold,
you're not taken seriously.*
–Rachel G.

©Skvoor

Coleman County sits just under two hundred miles southwest of Dallas in the middle-of-nowhere, Texas. On a scorching summer day in 1960-something, Jerry Harvey sat on his in-laws' porch playing dominoes on a folding card table. The temperature peaked at one-hundred and four degrees. Only a small fan, periodic wind gusts, and some cold lemonade mitigated the heat. But Jerry was nonetheless enjoying his game of dominoes, occasionally looking down at his feet to see fine grains of dust blowing across the deck and disappearing between the gaps in the floorboards.

Jerry's father-in-law cut into the peace of the Sunday afternoon by suggesting the family take a trip to get some dinner in Abilene. "What? Go to Abilene?" Jerry **thought to himself**.[21] He could hardly tolerate the idea of driving fifty-three miles back and forth in an un-air-conditioned Buick with his wife and in-laws. But before Jerry could grimace and furrow his brow, his wife chimed in: "Sounds like a great idea."

---

[21] Maybe the most important line in this whole story.

Jerry acquiesced, and then his mother-in-law voted yes by exclaiming she hadn't been to Abilene in quite a long time. So four family members ventured north that day based on a unanimous vote. And then Jerry's predictions of disaster came true: "The heat was brutal. We were coated with a fine layer of dust that was cemented with perspiration by the time we arrived." The foursome ate a mediocre meal and raced home to seek the relief of the porch fan.

With the purr of the fan the only noise breaking a silent night, Jerry decided to be sociable. "It was a great trip, wasn't it?" At that moment, full of frustration, suddenly no one feared judgment from the others. Jerry Harvey's mother-in-law voiced her irritation. She would rather have stayed home. "I wouldn't have gone if you hadn't all pressured me into it." Apparently, not having been to Abilene "in quite a long time" was her way of suggesting she could wait even longer.[22] Jerry fired back by expressing his contentment with the dominoes he'd been playing. His wife, with contempt for both of them, blamed her dad and Jerry. "It wasn't my idea."

"Hell!" Jerry's father-in-law shouted. "I never wanted to go to Abilene. I just thought you might be bored." The vote-out-loud had been four to zero for the trip. The unspoken vote resoundingly favored sitting on the porch all evening. But it was far too late. The trip to Abilene was five hours of their lives Jerry Harvey and his family would never get back. Jerry reflected in the aftermath:

---

[22]We've seen this type of communication before, a few pages back, in airplane cockpits.

After the outburst of recrimination we all sat back in silence. Here we were, four reasonably sensible people who, of our own volition, had just taken a 106-mile trip across a godforsaken desert in a furnace-like temperature through a cloud-like dust storm to eat unpalatable food at a hole-in-the-wall cafeteria in Abilene, when none of us had really wanted to go.

The **Abilene Paradox** is a classic. Harvey first told the story in 1974, touting "mutual agreement" as a detriment more insidious than even organizational conflict. He attributed the problems of sensible people's silence to fear: "Both research and experience indicate ostracism is one of the most powerful punishments that can be devised....the fear of taking risks that may result in *judgment* from others is at the core of the paradox."[23]

We can attribute failed family trips and disasters as monumental as the Watergate scandal to the specter of social judgment. When asked by a senator, "What on earth would it have taken to decide against the {Watergate} plan?" Jeb Magruder—a deputy to Nixon—responded under oath, "Not very much, sir." Herbert Porter, a partner in crime and colleague on the White House Staff, told the senate panel, "I drifted along...in all honesty, because of the fear of the group pressure that would ensue, of not being a team player." An autopsy of America's most damaging

---

[23] We took the liberty here of replacing the word "separation" with "judgment." Both are powerful, and either fits. Harvey focused on the deep impact of social isolation. Judgment creates a form of psychological isolation from others.

political moment revealed none of the players even considered the Watergate break-in a good idea. The President's men went to Abilene together. We're talking about grown adults and the diagnosis is peer pressure. These are shake-your-head moments. If fear of social disapproval weighs so mightily absent significant power dynamics, imagine how strong the metaphorical winds of judgment become when authority figures enter the mix.

Columbia Middle School sits quietly in small-town America, maybe a half-mile east of its namesake river in the center of Burbank, Washington. The school's gym looks like a small airplane hangar—built to hold no more than three hundred students at a time—but with a curving roof suited for the tail section of a mid-sized prop plane. On a November Saturday in 2008, even the meager set of bleachers, only ten rows high, looked relatively barren. A smattering of parents dotted the seats. Jason Crandall had moved from West Point, New York to Richland, Washington a few months earlier, and the dimly lit court in Burbank served as the site of his first-ever AAU basketball game. It was also the first time Jason played in a basketball contest I wasn't coaching.

Typically a solid shooter, maybe it was the gym lighting that threw him off; Jason missed a lot of shots that Saturday. About midway through the second quarter, he intercepted a pass near the opponent's three point line, raced to the opposite end, elevated a few inches, and misdirected a layup. The shot bounced too hard off the backboard and skidded across the front of the rim with a clang. As the ball fell into an opponent's hands, Jason looked into the stands for maybe the tenth time that morning. He'd glance, make eye contact, and refocus on the court. Then he'd look quickly again with a soft gaze aimed directly at me. Inside my head I was screaming at him, "Just play the game! Stop looking at me," but yelling out loud would only confirm what the other seven spectators were already thinking: "That boy's dad must whup him for every missed shot."

All fifth-grade long, Jason continued to look up into the stands when he made a mistake. There I was, smiling back at him. I'm far from the greatest sports parent in the world, but I support my kids. Missed shots never equal condemnation in our home.[24] My grown-up son claims not to remember his habit of looking to the bleachers. He's certainly moved past it. His teammates and he regularly challenge my decisions in the huddle these days. But he did it at eleven years old—all the time. No one can perform well like that—preoccupied with their leader's opinion. No one.

During the summer of 2014, Jason and his friends on Subway Select—a team I coached for five years— took the court against an acclaimed Seattle Rotary squad. Rotary boasts several NBA players among its alumni. At game time, the sixteen-and-under crew we faced ranked in the top fifteen in the country and had multiple players with college basketball futures.

Late in the contest, coming out of a timeout, I called an inbounds play. But Jason—offering a

---

[24] We save critiques for rare instances of lagging effort.

glancing wave of dismissal—rebuffed me. "We already got it." Sitting right behind him in a folding chair along the baseline was Bryant Moore of Pepperdine. Coach Moore would be impressed enough with Jason to give me a call the next day. Our conversation turned from basketball to leadership and character. "Yeah, I saw him wave you off that time. Ha! Figured he must be your son."

The thing is, the guys wave me off all the time. Coleman Sparling, our team captain, yells at me occasionally to be quiet with the refs. In one instance, with our team down by three points and just under a second left in the game, Coleman faced two free throws. As we stood in the huddle, I tried to be creative. Common basketball practice suggests Coleman make the first free throw and intentionally miss the second. Our guys would then aggressively chase an offensive rebound and try to tip the ball in for the tie. It's a long shot, but about the only chance to win in that situation. I had a different idea.

"Okay, how about if Coleman makes the second one, and we try to stop Rotary from getting the ball inbounds?" I couldn't finish my thought before Logan Adams, Scott Burge, Coleman, and Jason were shaking their heads and vilifying my suggestion. "No, coach. No way." It might sound like I have no control over the team. In some ways, that is true. But the thing is, they don't need me to control them. In fact, they hardly need me at all. Without doubt, the last thing Jason—or any of the guys—needs is to be thinking about my approval or disapproval when taking a shot, making a decision, or even calling an inbounds play.

There's a huge difference between the Jason who played in Burbank at eleven years old and the Jason who played against Seattle Rotary that summer. Little Jason worried about my judgment. World-beater Jason is out there carefree, giving it everything he has with complete focus. And there's no question which Jason you want on your team.

Fear of judgment impedes those we lead from saying what they think. What's true on the basketball court translates to your brainstorming sessions, your distribution center floors, and your customer service centers. Verbal or nonverbal disapproval extinguishes embers of dialogue that could become blazing bonfires of fearless communication. A leader's power douses those flames, and people's past experiences render innovations, improvements, feedback, and requests for help smoldering unacknowledged.

One of the great movie scenes of 2011 takes place early in the film version of Michael Lewis's *Moneyball*. Billy Beane—general manager of the Oakland A's—has hired Peter Brand to look at baseball scouting from an inventive, analytical perspective. Beane's a charismatic, determined executive motivated by his own past as a player. He's powerful, especially as far as Brand is concerned. Peter is new to the A's and new to providing input. Early on his first morning at work, Brand, simultaneously eager and apprehensive, approaches his general manager:

Peter Brand: I wanted you to see these player evaluations that you asked me to do.

Billy Beane: I asked you to do three.

Peter Brand: Yeah.

Billy Beane: To evaluate three players.

Peter Brand: Yeah.

Billy Beane: How many'd you do?

Peter Brand: Forty-seven.

Billy Beane: Okay.

Peter Brand: Actually, fifty-one. I don't know why I lied just then.

"*I don't know why I lied just then.*" Jonah Hill delivers the line with an impeccable lack of assurance. We know. Judgment is why Peter Brand lied, albeit briefly, little, and whitely. Asked to do three player evaluations, he overachieved by seventeen hundred percent. Although Beane could potentially see his initiative as a good thing, Brand wanted to soften the blow of his own ambition, and clearly desired to start on the right foot with his new boss.

The world's leading authority on psychological safety in teams, Amy Edmondson, unwraps the ways in which we prioritize our image and act to *save face*. People fear asking for help, admitting errors, or seeking feedback—even when it will benefit the organization—because these vulnerabilities may create "unfavorable impressions on people who influence decisions about promotions, raises, or project assignments."

Evaluation apprehension is "anxiety induced in a person performing some task while being observed by others and feeling anxious about being judged."[25] We mentioned previously the original findings from Gary Stasser's murder mystery experiment: people tend to share common knowledge, but are afraid of looking foolish by voicing things only they know. Or, as Edmondson points out, they may secretly fear sharing their "proprietary" information will lessen their own value (an adult version of keeping the homework answers to yourself). Others' silence may derive from a purer intent; some are simply reluctant to look like they're showing off.

These inhibitions are common human tendencies —tendencies amplified by the stinging, critical judgment of leaders. In his book *Social Intelligence*, Daniel Goleman illustrates the neurological mechanics at work. Social threats such as "fear of a leader's judgment or of seeming stupid" in front of others prompts cortisol levels (our stress hormone) to surge.[26] With increased cortisol levels come anxiety and a drop in performance. Our analytical capacity, creativity, and communication all shut down.

The thing about judging others is we're not really good at it. Leaders start by stereotyping. If we throw out the name Shameka Williams, your brain instantly creates a picture in your head. Not a conscious decision—your brain just does it. Got the image? Now if we throw out a different name, say, Sarah West,

---

[25] From the online *Oxford Dictionary of Psychology*.

[26] Goleman uses the word "teacher" and describes the scene as a classroom setting. We use "leader" here for effect.

your brain takes an entirely different snapshot. Can you see Sarah? One more name—Aradhya Subramani —and yet another photo flashes in your mind's eye. If next we asked you which woman is a stay-at-home mom, which is an IT executive at Google, and which plays in the WNBA, you would answer pretty easily. You might feel like a bad person, but you wouldn't have trouble categorizing the three fictitious women. It's how our brains work—almost by necessity. [27]

The story continues. Pretend Sarah approaches a bank. What does the bank look like? What color? How big? Where is it? What's the weather outside? Okay, now that you have your mental image of Sarah and her bank, Nobel Prize-winning economist Daniel Kahneman is going to make you feel inadequate. "If an earlier sentence had been, 'They were floating gently down the river,' you would have imagined an altogether different scene,"—a different sort of *bank,* Kahneman explains.

"Sarah approaches the bank" is an ambiguous statement. But in the absence of context, your mind created specificity. Of all the people who read SAY ANYTHING, only a handful will even have considered a river bank. Absent any actual knowledge of the three women, we created context surrounding Shameka, Sarah, and Aradhya.[28] How we process these names, and our failure to consider a river bank, are brain

---

[27] Remember: the more powerful leaders feel, the more they tend to stereotype. Hitler—a man of immense power—turned stereotypes into a national ethos.

[28] We're also guessing most people pictured a **white** mom, **Indian** IT worker, and **black** basketball player.

mechanics which replicate themselves with far more damaging ramifications every day.

One more play-along story: pretend Shameka, Sarah, and Aradhya are the three people assigned to your *Case of the Fallen Businessman* team. How do you decide whom you should listen to in order to solve the murder? Well, the person who talks first will immediately get a status bump. The best-looking of the three will have an upper hand. One of the women might mention her college degree, wear fashionable glasses, or smile kindly. A smile gains trust, but **friendliness is perceived as inversely related to competence**. A rounded chin also hints at questionable expertise. You will prefer Shameka because she's tall. Believe it or not, your judgment of her competence will depend on how good she is at basketball. Seriously. If she's an all-star in the WNBA, the *halo effect* explains you'll think of her as an all-star detective. We have difficulty parsing our judgments. The way we see a person in one regard (handsome, kind, athletic) translates to how we see him or her in all regards (smart, creative, analytical).

Assuming you even let anyone else talk (since you are the all-powerful leader), the status of the person who spoke first will soon be surpassed by the woman who speaks most often. Dominating conversational airtime results in high status. But again, beware the halo effect. It happens fast. If Aradhya's first comment is genius, she will do no wrong for the rest of the discussion, even if she babbles incoherently the next six times she opens her mouth. On the other hand—if

Sarah's first comment seems a little off-base, you will write her off. She could bring it like Sherlock Holmes for the next twenty minutes, but your brain will not get past that first moment of nonsense. "If we see a person first in a good light," suggests *The Economist*, "it is difficult to subsequently darken that light." The examples of how we judge swiftly, irrationally, and often incorrectly are almost endless. Deb Gruenfeld, a professor of leadership and organizational behavior at Stanford, tells us people evaluate others' competence in less than one-tenth of one-second.[29]

If you—the leader in our example—are anxious about the fight you had with your best friend, just watched a particularly disturbing movie the night prior, or are simply hungry and impatient, your three team members will suffer. Your sour mood will crush them. Mr. Guion's dead, and Eddie is going to walk. And truth be told, you don't really need to listen to these three anyway. *Confirmation bias* explains you'll be looking for input and evidence confirming what you already believe. Poor Sarah, with her stupid first comment, has both the halo effect and confirmation bias working against her. Oh yeah, and because the above statement is in bold, research demonstrates you're much more likely to believe it.[30]

Turns out leaders are also prone to bequeath higher status on those who speak more assertively. What if Shameka entered the discussion and

---

[29] Gruenfeld speaks from a lifetime of research on the topic of body language, judgment, and power.

[30] We use a fair amount of bold in the book—but mostly because it looks really sharp.

suggested she was torn about who she thought was guilty? She'd looked at all the evidence from a number of angles, and just wasn't sure. Would you value Shameka's candor? Reading this, right now, you might say "Yes." But if Shameka was instead providing input on how to discipline an employee, which venture to fund, or whether to sell a subsidiary, you'd write her off as indecisive. *"Come on, Shameka. Don't tell me you're not sure. Make a decision!"* We can hardly believe we are typing this. As a past college athlete and entrepreneur in one corner, and a former military officer in the other, what are we doing espousing the virtues of muddled indecision? After years of study and investigation, we've decided hearing the unfiltered, authentic thoughts of those you lead is more valuable than their presentation skills. Two researchers we will meet in a few pages make a point worth ample reflection:

> The culture of many organizations suppresses uncertainty and rewards behavior that ignores it...seldom do we see confidence as a warning sign —a hint that overconfidence, overoptimism, and other action-oriented biases may be at work. [31]

If Aradhya digs in with a proclamation that she has zero doubt Mrs. Guion committed the murder, we admire her fortitude. It's the real-world version of a Jedi mind-trick, and we can ascribe things such as the Challenger explosion and the failed launch of the Obamacare website to the derisive effects of demanding certainty and vilifying unfettered, yet

---

[31] Ovallo and Sibony.

authentic, doubt. What if, instead, some of the most powerful words in your organization were: *I'm not sure. I need help. I have a new idea...What if people could just communicate what they were really thinking, without having to run it through verbal Photoshop first?*

The more powerful leaders become, the more people we lead; and the more responsibility we take on, the more we judge based on fashionable eyewear, first comments, and Indian-sounding surnames. Thankfully there were no men in your murder mystery group, because guys who are dads get a status bump while moms in the workforce get downgraded.[32] It's all a mess really—just like these last many pages. As part of the human condition, all of us find arguments more favorable if we nod our head while the point is being made (regardless of an idea's validity). So nod your head as you read the rest of SAY ANYTHING. We'd appreciate it. The opposite is true when we shake our head in disagreement. In that case, we become skeptical as we listen. Humans do our thinking with our bodies as well as our brains.

Let's slow down for a second and wrap our heads around everything we just laid out. At the outset of SAY ANYTHING, our Steven Hauschka Seattle Seahawks example probably annoyed some San Francisco 49er fans. In a similar fashion, if you're a financial advisor touting your stock-picking skills, you might want to skip the next couple pages...

---

[32] Research from Amy Cuddy of Harvard Business School.

Back when I was in business school, my finance professor, Peter DeMarzo, told the class something that forever changed my investment strategies: the S&P 500 beats 80% of all mutual funds every year. (Now read that bolded sentence again while nodding your head.) But what about those funds with incredible track records, DeMarzo asked rhetorically? Then he wowed the classroom:

> Mutual Fund companies start new funds all the time. If a fund underperforms in its first or second year, they shut it down, or at least stop advertising it. If a fund beats the S&P, they keep it going. Thirteen years later, at least one of their funds will be standing. That's the one they are touting.

Daniel Kahneman—the gentleman with the Nobel Prize in economics we introduced a few pages back—explains, "The evidence from more than fifty years of research is conclusive: for a large majority of fund managers, the selection of stocks is more like rolling the dice than like playing poker." Unless the person picking your stocks is Warren Buffett, you'd probably be better off investing that commission. And, your investment practices mirror all the things leaders do when they judge their people's contributions to team dialogue. If your broker started off with a great first year, you fell prey to the halo effect. He (and we use "he" on purpose, because that's our mental image), gained high status and became an indispensable part of your financial security. When year one went well, it wasn't *good* luck. You were a genius for hiring the right advisor. Then in years three and four, when things nose-dived, you wrote it off as bad luck. "He'll recover his old form," you told yourself. If the opposite occurred—if your financial advisor had a bad first year—well then, you probably fired him and found a new one in year two. The fired guy moved on and racked up double-digit returns for the next decade. When you heard about his success, you wrote it off as lucky and uncovered some evidence suggesting stock prognosticators don't know much anyway (confirmation bias)—except yours of course.

We do this with our own amateur financial endeavors, but investors in Silicon Valley fare no better. Amy Cuddy of Harvard explains, "The success of venture-capital pitches to investors apparently turns, in fact, on nonverbal factors like how comfortable and charismatic you are. The predictors of who actually gets the money are all about how you present yourself, and nothing to do with content." Sounds a lot like rolling the dice.

This is how we treat our people. As leaders, we are not evil monsters (most of us anyway). Our days are busy and stressed, and our jobs require we act quickly. We need our go-to direct reports, and we don't have time for nonsense and silly ideas. Consider everything we have talked about in this rant on judgment, and let's tie it together with three super-enlightening bits of research related to people speaking fearlessly…

1. Professor Gruenfeld of Stanford tells us, "Whether an argument is persuasive is rarely a reflection of its quality; many arguments

aren't even heard until the right person makes them." We mix all these things together—our stereotypes, our halo effects, our biases, judgments, and humanity—and we rank people consciously and subconsciously. We accord them status. Undoubtedly you've had an experience where someone else shared an idea you'd brought up before. Then Mike or Amanda says it two weeks later. Voilà, the boss thinks it's great.[33] (Reminder—this book is not about your boss. This book is about you and the way you lead. So—what potentially game-changing ideas are you dismissing because they aren't coming from the "right person"?)

2. Amy Cuddy (the aforementioned Harvard expert) has spent years studying the dynamics of power, body language, and influence. She explains, "People make inferences of competence based on how dominant someone appears." Multiple sources of research confirm those who talk the most, talk first, and talk assertively gain the highest status in a group. These are the supposed "right people."

    BUT...

---

[33] Reminder—this book is not about your boss. This book is about you and the way you lead. So—what potentially game-changing ideas are you dismissing because they aren't coming from the *"right person"*?

3. According to introversion guru Susan Cain, "There's zero correlation between being the best talker and having the best ideas." This doesn't mean people who talk a lot have poor ideas; it simply means their ideas are no better or worse than the ideas of those who are saying little. But, not all the people saying little are innately introverted. Many are extroverts outside of the workplace. They're not speaking up because they've been suffocated by their leaders, bitten by past experiences, and frozen by the fear of judgment and disapproval. They've become de facto introverts in order to survive in their organizations. We, as leaders, are both failing to draw out ideas from our introverts and, at the same time, shutting up our extroverts.

Leaders listen to their high-status people
(and often don't even hear anyone else).

Those who talk well, early, a lot,
and loudly earn high status.

There's zero correlation between
someone being a good talker and the
quality of his or her ideas.

Uh oh.

The previous twenty pages are erratic, fast-paced, and maybe even headache-inducing. We get that. But it's important information to grasp if you're to get anything out of this book. Daniel Kahneman's *Thinking, Fast and Slow* is four hundred and eighteen pages long. We enjoyed the much-shorter *Blink* by Malcolm Gladwell, but some consider *Blink* dry, and those with letters after their name (like Matt) label it pseudoscience authored by a talented but non-expert pop writer. There are books and books and books and books, and Harvard Business Review articles, and Fast Company features, and TED lectures, and still more books full of more mind-works than all of us could ever digest, much less put to practical use. Research on the halo effect has been around for nearly a hundred years. During that time, we haven't evolved beyond it, learned to avoid it, or implemented procedures to call it out when we see it. If you watch late-night television, you understand only a sliver of our population can name the standing vice president or identify Oklahoma on a map—the halo effect and its many wily cousins are top-of-mind for almost no one.

In the end, leading well is hard work. We generally aren't good at it. There's a lot working against us, including our own minds and emotions. You can read all the books in the world, and you'll never fix all your own biases—those biases that make your people's cortisol levels rise and impede open communication. But we can get better at recognizing and mitigating them by enabling others to speak up and call us out. Once we've done that, the next step is a transition to inspiring ideas, cultivating candor, and forging a culture of fearless communication...[34]

Also a bank...

---

[34] Real bank ©Roberto Giovannini. Piggy bank ©Dvmsimages

THE
GROUNDWORK

7. THE POSSIBILITIES

If leadership is about getting people to do what you want done, then you are the limit of the team's potential.
—Pat Bettin, University of Washington Foster School of Business

By the time Abraham Lincoln floated the idea of an Emancipation Proclamation to his closest advisors, he'd already made up his mind. He didn't open it up for a cabinet vote, and he entertained no discussion. Historian Doris Kearns Goodwin suspects Lincoln wanted little confusion about who owned the consequences. "He welcomed their suggestions after they heard what he had to say," writes Goodwin, "but he wanted them to know that he 'had resolved upon this step, and had not called them together to ask their advice.'" Such a heavy-handed declaration constituted a rarity for the interpersonally gifted Lincoln. Kearns, after all, titled her voluminous biography of the man *Team of Rivals*. Lincoln's humility engendered a robustness of commentary rarely seen at such high levels of power. So despite having already made the emancipation decision, he subsequently engaged his team in healthy debate about the *how* of the proclamation. William Seward, Secretary of State, voiced concern about timing. In the summer of 1862, the Union's war effort had hit bottom. Seward believed a July announcement would convey desperation rather than calculation. Or in other words, he told the President of the United States of America, who had already made up his mind on the matter: "This is not the right decision, right now." Lincoln listened.

Seward didn't just have a critique; he had a suggestion. The Secretary recommended Lincoln wait until the Union achieved a military victory—make the emancipation official in the wake of success. President Lincoln delivered the Emancipation Proclamation two months later, following the September 17th, 1862 Battle of Antietam—a Union victory (sort of). The adept timing of the announcement dissuaded the British and French governments from officially recognizing the Confederacy. Ultimately, a case can be made that Seward's suggestion—and Lincoln's resulting delay of the announcement—created a major strategic shift in the course of the Civil War.

Leaders such as Lincoln who equip and inspire others to speak fearlessly reap rewards on the level of historically strategic. Second lieutenants in the army benefit in smaller ways....

I forget who taught me about the tiny violin—the official musical instrument of first-world problems—but it's become my daughter's favorite in the string family. I pull it out maybe five or six times each year —my right forefinger strumming at the base of my thumbnail—to metaphorically provide musical ambiance and dramatization when she is whining. "The world's tiniest violin, Mackenzie, playing just for you." Get out your tiny violin, because I'm about to share the hardest year of my professional life: 1997.

On paper, a U.S. Army tank battalion support platoon consists of around eighty soldiers and forty vehicles. Responsibilities range from transporting food, fuel, and ammunition to the front-line tank companies to replenishing, monitoring, and distributing a variety of products classified as hazardous material. Upon taking the reins of the support unit, I remember discovering fifty percent of the platoon had no license to operate the cargo and fuel trucks. That didn't stop them from driving, just from driving legally. Anytime we set rubber on a state or national highway, our drivers were required to affix labels indicating the HAZMAT classification of their load. Not only was our platoon void of anyone knowledgeable in proper signage, we didn't even have the placards. There were no systems for accountability of hundreds of thousands of dollars' worth of tools, tents, camouflage nets, and other equipment. I remember the platoon sergeant quipped:

The fuel specialists in this platoon? They all want to be sitting on an airfield servicing choppers. The transportation specialists in this platoon? They all want to be long-haul trucking for the corps headquarters. The tankers in this platoon? They all want to be on tanks. Basically, no one wants to be here.

The officer in this platoon? Cue tiny violin. I remember one night at Yakima Training Center the battalion commander summoned me to the tank firing line at the multi-purpose range complex, which was probably a twenty-five-minute Humvee drive up a winding dirt road. I registered an impressive ten to twelve major mistakes per day that winter and spent the whole ride wondering what new disaster proved catastrophic enough for the commander to allocate time chewing me out. I expected to lose my job.

My driver pulled our vehicle into a makeshift parking spot just outside a drab cement building. It looked eerily like something the CIA would use to interrogate a suspect in the Middle East. I walked through twenty feet of total darkness and reached my hand out to turn the knob. I opened the door and inside were only four people: Lieutenant Colonel Campbell, the sergeant major, and two soldiers standing stiffly and silently. Twin light bulbs hanging nakedly from the ceiling provided dim illumination on the moonless night. The booming sound of an M1A1 firing into the distance broke the silence as I stepped toward my battalion commander. The soldiers' eyes stared straight through me as I walked up and rendered a salute. "Sir, Lieutenant Crandall reports as ordered."

"These two knuckleheads," the colonel barked with a hint of disbelief, "drove their fuel truck off a twenty-foot embankment. It's sitting on the side of a hill right now, about to fall into a canyon. They are lucky to be alive." There were moments—like this one —when I just wanted my army career to end in a glorious heap of destruction. That seemed preferable to another day.

Specialists Turner and Mendoza had been going forty miles per hour, in the pitch black, on a thirty-foot-wide dirt trail. They never saw the turn. Their tanker truck, filled to capacity with twenty-five hundred gallons of gas, flew (literally) off the road and plunged its nose into a large piece of earth. The two had decided not to wear their night vision goggles as they drove. Lieutenant Colonel Campbell scolded me:

> I put you in this job to get this stuff squared away. It's getting worse, not better. I don't have time to worry about a couple drivers in your platoon. There are six hundred other soldiers for me to concern myself with. Do your job! I just can't...I just...get out of here.

And he sent me on my way. The blow could have been harder. Maybe he knew I was trying—sinking, but trying. I remember he told me when I started the job, "I need you to fix discipline and fix morale." So far, I had done neither.

I found out on the return ride to our perimeter that Turner and Mendoza decided to leave their night vision equipment back at Ft. Lewis—for the whole six-week training cycle. "They didn't have any batteries," Turner shrugged in a voice belying agreement with his own rationalization. That night, we had been about five feet of hillside away from two guys tumbling to a fiery death. We followed up the next day with an inventory of our "sensitive items," and came up ten short. Commanders will shut down an entire training operation for one missing item. We were missing ten—thousands of dollars worth.

I stressed a bit and yelled a little. Behind my back, I'm sure guys rolled their eyes. We located all the missing items back at Ft. Lewis (where Turner and others had left them), but the damage was done. I'd doled out a lot of judgment and anger. I remember sitting in a port-a-potty in the middle of a barren landscape just a few days later. The wind was whipping the twenty-degree temperatures down to zero. I looked up to my right. Scrawled in pencil on the inside of the port-a-potty wall were words I can still picture:

LT crandle is a punk-ass-bitch!

I learned a lot about myself that year.[35]

Fast-forward five months and our battalion was midway through a month-long deployment to the National Training Center at Ft. Irwin, California. Before September 11, 2001, rotations to NTC were pinnacle moments in an army unit's time together. Evaluations, promotions, and bragging rights all rested on this simulated combat exercise. With the exception of four Blitzkrieg-like days in Iraq, the late 1990s were two and a half decades removed from any

---

[35] And, yes, whoever wrote it spelled my name wrong.

real combat for U.S. armed forces.[36] I think a lot of us believed our army might never see war again (hopefully). We pretended NTC was it.

The previous six pages of describing how hard that year was provide context for what Sergeant Davies offered up to me on a stress-filled day in June. The desert heat pounded my face. I had dirt caked behind my ears and sweat running down my cheeks. Behind me were three metal steps, leading up to the door of a white, square building—like a box, about the size of a booth at the fair. That white container was our company headquarters. Davies had knocked on the door and interrupted my fuel forecasting to share something important.

I treasure some of the relationships I made in the army. I still laugh out loud when I think of the thick and biting sarcasm my diminutive gunner—Sergeant Kelly Wortman—spread across the small interior of our tank turret as we waited patiently for the enemy to crest a far-off hill. But that year as support platoon leader proved so stressful and mentally taxing, I regretfully didn't carry any of the relationships beyond my time in the role. Of all the guys in the platoon, however, I respected the professionalism and drive of Sergeant Davies the most. So when he knocked on the door, the disruption irritated me a bit, but I gave him a moment.

"Sir," he said in a tone both mildly unsure and wholly compassionate, "the guys are talking." The

---

[36] Blitzkrieg is the German word for "lightning war." It's a burst of intense, rapid, but powerful attacks. The first Gulf War took place over ninety-six hours in January of 1991.

sergeant clearly took inventory of his thoughts and measured the impact of what came next.

You're losing respect within the platoon, sir. We've all noticed you're spending a lot of time around the commander, over here in the headquarters. You're even sleeping over here, sir. This isn't where you should be, L-T. I really think when you bunk up tonight, you should come back and be with the platoon.

Wha-bam! Pow! Boom! Of all the things anyone has said to me during my years as a leader (at least to my face), that one hit with the most force, stung the hardest, and came at the least opportune time in terms of my own confidence. For months I'd been taking body blows such as Turner and Mendoza's Evel Knievel impression at Yakima and the graffiti on the port-a-potty wall. I spent ten minutes staring straight ahead at a brick wall one afternoon, listening to the captain tell me just how much I sucked. One of the guys forgot to put a chock-block behind the tire of his cargo truck when he went inside for lunch. My boss seriously threatened to end my stint as platoon leader right then and there—because of a chock block.

What Sergeant Davies pointed out resonated in the worst way possible. In the moments I feel alive as a leader, my spirit revs because I'm serving, caring, and making people's lives better. Whether with an army unit, a basketball team, or a classroom full of students, leadership—to me—is about getting the most out of others. And Sergeant Davies had the gall to come over, knock on the door, let me know "the guys" had lost respect for me, and suggest I do something to fix it—something like placing my sleeping bag down next to theirs that night? He had the gumption to suggest I was getting nothing out of these guys at all?

Abso-freaking-lutely he did. When my gut recovered and my throbbing ego subsided, I reluctantly thanked him. This squad leader, a couple rungs down the chain of command, was the only one who cared enough about me and enough about the platoon to Say Anything to his leader—anything at all.

Therein lies the opportunity of this entire book and a new way of thinking about the valuable insights of those we serve. When we cultivate candor, ideas thrive, sacred cows die, decisions improve, and lieutenants have opportunities to regain the respect of their soldiers.[37]

If you're not ready for the Sergeant Davies of the world to cut open your chest cavity and remove the tumor of your own failure, we understand. But anesthetic soft-talk is the arch-enemy of true leadership. We envision ourselves—the leaders—as the ones who must talk straight. We're not arguing against that. But flip that notion upside down and focus on those you lead speaking candidly to you. Everything you hear will make your organizations and you better. It may sting at first, but the advantages of open communication are (ironically, given present context) beyond debate.

---

[37] That very day, I went back and refocused on the platoon. I thank Sergeant Davies from the bottom of my heart.

Dan Ovallo from McKinsey & Company and Olivier Sibony from the University of Sydney investigated 1,048 business decisions over five years. During the course of their research, they made countless inquiries into decision-making processes, asking the following questions (among others):

> Did discussion include perspectives that contradicted the senior executive's point of view?

> Did [the executives] elicit participation from a range of people who had a different view of the decision?

The pair also exhaustively studied the level and quality of analytical rigor contributing to each of the thousand-plus decisions. The Ovallo-Sibony research zeroed in on a profound conclusion all leaders should take counsel of:

> ### Process mattered more than analysis by a factor of six.[38]

When launching products, acquiring businesses, altering corporate structure, or deciding who to hire and fire, analysis matters; but the benefits of debate, discussion, skepticism, and scrutiny matter six times more. Absent an authentic and vibrant process, "good

---

[38] Thanks to Chip and Dan Heath and their outstanding book *Decisive* for alerting us to this research. We recommend all the Heath brothers' titles—also *Made to Stick* and *Switch*.

analysis in the hands of good managers, argue Ovallo and Sibony, "won't naturally yield good decisions."

Jim Collins echoes this idea in *Good to Great*: "You absolutely cannot make a series of good decisions without confronting the brutal facts." Leaders must establish "a climate where the truth is heard" to overcome the the types of biases and blind spots we've already explored.

Turns out there's yet another blind spot—a big one: people tend to harbor a hidden bias against creativity. Almost no one will say it out loud, but research suggests it's close to universally true. We prefer known solutions, especially in times of uncertainty.[39] Ironically, it's at times of uncertainty that creative solutions are often most needed. Leaders will opt for slightly new ideas, but don't go all "Earth revolves around the sun" on us or you're bound to get shot down. "American culture worships creativity," opined *The Atlantic* in October 2014, "but mostly in the abstract." In order to gain idea acceptance, the magazine recommended that people "frame new ideas as old ideas—to make your creativity seem, well, not quite so creative." Not bad advice for those suffering under the thumb of tone-deaf leadership, but not the advice of this book. We remind you once again, this book is about you and your leadership. Stop holding your people prisoner to the idea that they must present all thoughts and ideas *the right way* —that is, the way that keeps you feeling comfortable.

---

[39] Research from Mueller, Melwani, and Goncalo.

In his book *Drive*, Daniel Pink teaches that mental parameters such as, in this instance, trying to find the right way to say something to your boss, significantly hinder creative thinking. Communication is hard enough when people say what they mean (think back to Daniel Kahneman's bank example). So as long as the people you lead are focused on cracking your language code—or trying to say things the way they imagine you want to hear them—they're no doubt giving you a lot of crappy suggestions. And this forces you to tighten the reins even more, right? Of course, you have to micromanage because your people can't think for themselves—and it's true, they can't. Not under the scrutiny and fear of having to articulate their own ideas into your own personal safe language for them to even be heard.

Instead of responding based on your own discomfort and uncertainty when you hear a new idea, force yourself to shut up and not immediately object to anything. Just listen. Take a deep breath, bite your tongue, be the leader, and listen to what your people are saying. Take a deep breath, bite your tongue, be the leader, and listen to what your people are saying. Yes, we wrote that sentence twice on purpose. Listen, not while preparing a rebuttal in your head, but listen so you hear. In executive coaching terms, it's called active listening. You'll hear amazing "new" ideas. Oh yeah, and your people will respect you more and be eager to share all the awesome things they've kept locked in their mental vault for years because they've been afraid to speak candidly.

Sometime prior to 1993, Pacific Power and Light gathered a team to address the debilitating effects of inclement weather.[40] Freezing temperatures often conspired with the moisture of the Pacific Northwest to leave power lines cocooned in ice. When harsh conditions persisted over a matter of days, the weight of the ice would cause the lines to stress and ultimately snap. The hazard forced Pacific Power to send its workers into the field to climb the poles and, with long hooks, shake the lines. It was both a nasty and a dangerous job.

Several attempts to solve the case of the icy power lines proved fruitless. The company eventually brought some of the front-line technicians into the brainstorming mix. Intimidated, many of these workers sat quietly and listened to the ideas of others. But during a break, a Pacific Power executive overheard one of the company's operators complain to his buddy: "I hate that crazy job. Last week, I fell off the slippery pole. When I landed, I was peering into the eyes of an enormous black bear. He did not seem to like me invading his territory."

"We should just train the bears to climb the poles and shake the ice off," his friend responded, "black bears are best."[41]

---

[40] We traced the story to author Elaine Camper in a paper dated April 2, 1993. Her wording suggests it occurred "a number of years" before that. The company is now named Pacific Power and owned by Warren Buffett's Berkshire Hathaway.

[41] The black bear quote is entirely for fans of *The Office*. You can't spend months writing a book and not have a little fun.

In a meeting room full of executives they did not trust, these two hands-on professionals remained silent. But during a bathroom break, they became the key to steamrolling an entire morning of barricaded creativity. The Pacific Power manager who overheard the idea asked friend number two to share what he had said during the break. He figured it to be mostly nonsensical but thought it might lubricate some further discussion. On cue, the rest of the group laughed when the gentleman suggested his bear-training technique. Full-blown judgment and disapproval immediately took hold.

Either feeling uncomfortable with the laughter directed at his colleague, or genuinely attempting to forward the dialogue, a different line worker raised his hand. "It might be tough to train the bears to do that, but what if we put honey pots at the top of the electric poles? The bears would climb the poles to get the honey and knock the ice off the wires."

The discussion gained a slight tone of sincerity and a manager asked: "How is that better than what we have now? We'd have to get the honey pots on top of the poles."

A crusty, senior line worker chimed in with a voice of indignation. "Our execs are always flying around in their fancy helicopters. Why don't we just use the choppers for some good and fly around placing honey pots on poles?" Smatters of laughter bounced around the room until a secretary spoke up. "I was a nurse's aide in Vietnam. Casualties were always flying into our field hospital on helicopters. The downwash from the helicopter blades threw everything around. The dust and the debris would almost blind us. Why don't we just fly the helicopters over the power lines and let the rotors knock the ice off." From bears to honey pots to helicopters, a secretary at Pacific Power and Light—a woman willing to Say Anything in that moment—crafted a solution that a company used for decades.

Former Microsoft CEO Steve Ballmer predicted the iPhone would never gain traction. Decca Records, in a first-ever audition, famously told the Beatles that groups like theirs had gone out of style. In 1927, Harry Warner of Warner Bros. Pictures asked, "Who the hell wants to hear actors talk?" Our nation was only one peer-pressure-busting statement away from never having experienced Watergate. Executives at ABC shook their heads in amusement when Lloyd Braun first proposed the television series *Lost*.[42] You might have heard E. L. James self-published *Fifty Shades of Grey* after widespread rejection, but did you know Mark Twain self-published *The Adventures of Huckleberry Finn*? Every studio in Hollywood rejected *Raiders of the Lost Ark*. As leaders, we need as much help as possible. If we don't capitalize on those around us, our own abilities and ideas become the maximum capacity of the teams we ostensibly lead. **We need creative ideas, slaps in the face, and warnings of impending doom**. We need to listen, and we need to listen *well* so our people break through the aforementioned obstacles, believe in their ideas, and start speaking up.

---

[42] Considered by many to be one of the top few television series of all time, its ending notwithstanding.

My dad was 5′7″ and said only a handful of words on most days of the week. My mom worked evenings as I was growing up, and my closest sibling left for college when I was ten, so Dad and I spent a lot of time together—just the two of us. He would come home from work, change into his grey fleece sweatpants and white t-shirt, and put on his brown tennis shoes with velcro straps where the laces should have been. Practical but lame. I remember he always left his work socks on inside the tennis shoes. I swore I'd never replicate that sort of old-man dork-factor. Such a lack of fashion was just plain lazy (or at least I thought so until I turned about forty).

My mom usually made some food for us and left it in the fridge. After Dad warmed it, we'd sit at the table and just kind of look at each other, or the wall, or I'd hide my peas under my mashed potatoes. Then we would transition to the TV room where Dad kicked back in his recliner and tuned into *Three's Company* or *Knight Rider*. My dad pretty much watched whatever and seemingly forgot I was there. There wasn't a lot of trash on network television at the time; I survived *Dallas* and *Dynasty* mostly unscathed. Point being, we didn't talk a whole lot, Dad and me. Friday nights were about *The Love Boat* and *Fantasy Island*: uninterrupted.

Not gifted with gab, Loo Crandall demonstrated his love by letting me caddy on Saturday mornings and coaching my soccer team in the fall. When the sixth-grade season came around, I was fresh off a week at Northwest Soccer Camp on Whidbey Island.

My skills—and my head—had expanded during camp. At one of our first practices, Dad decided we'd work on corner kicks. We were on the strikingly beautiful dirt field at my future middle school. Our team of fifteen twelve-year-olds gathered behind the corner flag in a semi-circle. My dad, who never played soccer himself growing up, arched his small frame over the ball and told our team: "I want you to lean over it like this and lift it up in the air." Wisely, he didn't try to show us; he simply told us. Apparently, I'd partially recovered from the Mrs. Patterson pre-school traffic-light trauma, because I interrupted my dad and smugly informed my mates, "You don't lean over it to get it up in the air. They taught us at soccer camp you lean back like a pitching wedge and *lift* it into the air!" My dad didn't call me a liar, but he did tell me to be quiet. "Let's try it my way for now," he instructed the team.

The next thing I remember about that frame of my life, I'm standing in our garage pouring dry dog food into a rectangular orange bucket on the ground. It was a forty-pound bag (for a one-hundred and eighty pound dog), so I was exerting some decent effort to prepare the daily meal for Clyde. The door leading from the two-car garage to the kitchen was six inches to the left of my head. I saw it pop open, then noticed my dad standing above me. "About the corner kicks...I looked it up. You were right, and I was wrong." He closed the door and walked back inside. I don't remember for how long, but I stood still in the quiet of that moment considering his words. Then I finished pouring the dog food. The next day at practice my father humbly informed our team, "I was wrong about the corner kicks. You need to lean back, like Doug said, to get the ball in the air."

Create a world where the people you lead can Say Anything, and the possibilities are innumerable. My dad died over a decade ago. I told the corner kick story as part of his eulogy. He probably wouldn't have had any recollection of the incident, but that simple moment changed my life. When we empower, when we withhold judgment, and when we encourage others to speak fearlessly through our words and actions big and small, we not only cultivate better ideas, decisions, and organizations, we also foster ownership, build leaders, and make people whole. My dad was no slouch. He served in the Marines, graduated from West Point, received his diploma from Eisenhower, earned his MBA, became a vice president at Boeing, raised a tight-knit family, and loved his wife for forty-eight years. But none of that made him too important to let his smartass son Say Anything, and our team's corner kicks (and my childhood) prospered as a result.

Our own kids sometimes speak to my wife and me like I talked to my dad. Timmy, our youngest, followed in his older brother Jason's footsteps and took up basketball. Unlike Jason, Timmy never looks to the sideline when I attend his games. He doesn't really care what I think. I mentioned in the footnotes several chapters back that we save sports critiques in our family for rare instances of lagging effort. There was a Sunday afternoon where Timmy sort of floated along through the first half of a game. He was jogging up and down the court, and his defense lacked intensity. Few things will accelerate the pulse of a basketball coach (or overbearing father) more quickly than lackadaisical defense. I turned to my daughter, Mackenzie, midway through the first half and grumbled, "What's the deal with your brother? Look at him. He has his back to the ball and he's completely lost his man."

At halftime, I did what no parent should ever do. I called Timmy over and told him to get his head in the game. "Play some defense. Show some heart." He improved in the second half and even mustered a few steals en route to a win. Later that night, on the way home from celebrating his 12th birthday at Dick's Drive-In, I broached the subject of proper defensive technique. My sermon lasted for about three minutes, during which I told him, "Don't turn your back to the ball" at least seven times. "It's about giving it one-hundred percent. You're capable of playing great defense. Stuff like turning your back to the ball is all about effort." The conversation slowed, and Timmy got just a little bit angry—not "my brother took the remote control" angry, but he was clearly agitated. Finally he let it out. "Okay, but I don't even know what you're talking about when you say 'don't turn your back on the ball!'"

The curse of knowledge hit me over the head.[43] I'd forgotten what it's like not to know and lectured Timmy in gibberish as we passed several mileposts. There's so much power in anyone—youngest kid,

---

[43] The curse of knowledge—something else we learned from Chip and Dan Heath—describes those moments where we forget what it's like "not to know." The original research came from Elizabeth Newton, a Stanford psychologist.

janitor, new hire, rookie, private first class, or co-pilot —saying anything. Anyone. Anything. If Timmy doesn't speak up in that moment, I assume he got the message. Meanwhile, everything I said was lost on him. I wasted my time. I wasted his time—all unwittingly. Performance won't improve, and frustration will mount. The next time I see Timmy turn his back to the ball, I assume he blew me off. **Leaders often mistake a lack of clarity for defiance.** I then conclude he lacks respect or just doesn't care. The situation spirals downward at an accelerated rate. Three months later, I fire him. Maybe four. And while I can't fire Timmy from our family, you get the point. Maybe I get lucky and none of this happens. But I doubt it. Timmy's willingness to speak up saved me in that moment. If I reflect and learn from it, it will save me in the future as well.

The Facebook campus in Menlo Park, California looks one part company headquarters and two parts Disneyland's Main Street USA. There's free food everywhere: at the pizza place, Mexican restaurant, hamburger joint, and daily buffet. Walk northwest from the restaurants and you can find a barber shop, dry cleaner, dessert stand, and outdoor refrigerators filled with soda, sports drinks, and water. It was somewhere on site in this pseudo-amusement park— just steps away from more free snacks and a graffiti wall where employees write whatever they want in permanent marker— that we encountered a character named Andrew Bosworth. "Boz," as others call him, started shaving his head during his twenties—which was probably only a few years before we met him. He looks like a cross between a linebacker and, um, well, actually he just looks like a linebacker. Oddly enough, his name sounds as if he once played in the NFL.

While a Harvard undergrad student majoring in computational neurobiology, Boz served as the teaching assistant in an artificial intelligence elective. Mark Zuckerberg was a sophomore in the class, but rarely showed up. He was busy working on some "outside project." A couple years later, after a stint at Microsoft, Bosworth found his way to Facebook and spent nine months inventing the News Feed feature and trying to impress Zuckerberg, his new boss (and former student).

Boz has been at Facebook since close to the beginning. He considers himself the social network's unofficial historian; he even takes pictures at company events. Although he was Director of Engineering at the time we met him, we'd never encountered anyone with such a firm grasp on an organization's *culture*. He explained exhaustively, "At Facebook, the only knowledge we trust is knowledge we've experienced on our own." They have no standard operating procedures, no set way of doing things, and no one is compelled to trust anyone's argument about tried-and-true methods. The only thing you can't say at Facebook is: "That's just the way we do it." Fittingly, Boz has a tattoo just above his left wrist that reads *veritas*—the Latin word for *truth*. "I have always just believed in transparency and honesty," he once divulged to the L.A. Times. "That's a big part of who I am as a person. I wear my heart on my sleeve." The culture of Facebook seems to reflect the personality of Andrew Bosworth as much as it does Mark Zuckerberg or Sheryl Sandberg. He told us at the end of our time together, "There's a measurable cost and an immeasurable benefit of having people closely connected by this deep-seated belief of questioning anything." Just a few minutes before we met Boz, a director of product marketing told us, "We are generally fearless about having the hard conversations."

We are not vouching for Facebook. We know no more than what we heard over the course of a half-day. We will bear witness however to the incredible intellect, charisma, and grasp of corporate mindset displayed by Bosworth. With him as a driving force, they seem to have constructed a culture of candor from the bottom up. Anyone can Say Anything, and if it makes sense in the present, they will kill projects, launch new ones, and turn one-hundred eighty degrees. It's not for the faint of heart, but it's effective.

The last person we met that day was Sheryl Sandberg, Chief Operating Officer of Facebook, best-selling author of *Lean In,* and billionaire. Sandberg had a singular leadership lesson she chose to share: "Understand it's really hard to get people to tell you the truth."

Let's turn the page and start the journey toward making that happen...

8. CENTER OF GRAVITY

We are determined that before the sun sets on this terrible struggle, Our flag will be recognized throughout the world as a symbol of freedom on the one hand and of overwhelming force on the other.

-General of the Army George C. Marshall

Lieutenant Colonel (Retired) Antulio Echevarria is one of a handful of Princeton-trained PhDs to serve in the U.S. Army in the last thirty years. "Tony" taught history at West Point, was a visiting research fellow at Oxford, and serves as the editor of *Parameters,* the U.S. Army's version of *Harvard Business Review*. Having spent much of his adult life studying the writings of Carl von Clausewitz, Echevarria might be the only person in the military who fully understands the Center of Gravity concept. He's written on it extensively, trying to tie together disparate views. The U.S. Marines, Navy, Army, and Air Force all subscribe to different definitions of Clausewitz's second most famous contribution to modern military thinking.[44]

Echevarria uses original text to clarify the idea—which is no small task considering the 19th century version of Clausewitz's six-hundred-page treatise *On War* was written in unedited and dialectically nuanced German. For the handful of scholars who dig

---

[44] The first being his contention that war is an "extension of policy (or politics) by other means."

into such sacred military texts, it's much like interpreting books of the Bible. Translation of individual words matters. The seven or eight people on the planet who understand enough to dissect Clausewitz's original writings end up arguing among themselves.

Why does it matter really—what Carl von Clausewitz meant when he used the words "center of gravity" circa 1820? It matters because our senior military leaders view monumental strategic decisions through the lens of Clausewitz's writings. In military universities across the services, the future flag officers of our respective forces spend months, or even years, honing their own perspectives on what someone like Clausewitz intended when he wrote *On War*. Their opinions are ultimately shaped by experts like Tony Echevarria. The lieutenant colonel didn't make his mark on the front lines of combat. Instead, he influenced influencers in the likes of the Pentagon.

As a cadet at West Point, I actually spent an eight-week summer internship in the iconic building, working in the office of European and NATO affairs. One afternoon, an older man in a dark suit stopped me in the expansive Pentagon hallways. "What are you doing here?" he asked. I was wearing a uniform we called "white over gray"—a short-sleeved, collared shirt with polyester gray pants. Up top on the shoulders there were gray epaulettes. The pants had a one-inch thick black stripe running down the side. I'd get a lot of glances in this uniform. Some of them came from people who recognized my get-up and others from people thanking me for attending to the elevator. It was unusual to be stopped by a civilian.

The distinguished-looking man was tall, lanky, and sported a pair of jumbo eyeglasses.[45]

"Well, sir," I replied confidently to his inquiry, "I'm a cadet from West Point." I smiled inside saying that. People in this building loved cadets. "Yes, I know *what* you are," he replied in a somewhat stodgy fashion. "But *why* are you here?" I paused. He didn't.

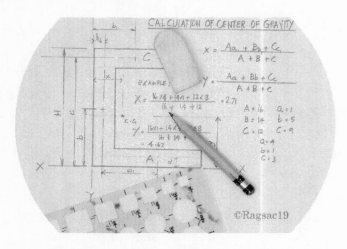

"I'm General Goodpaster. I used to be superintendent of the academy." He didn't mention the part about also commanding NATO. I got the impression General Goodpaster quietly disapproved of my presence inside his head: *Never would a cadet have been wasting his time at the Pentagon when I was in charge.* I certainly knew of General Goodpaster. His first and middle names were Andrew and Jackson, for goodness sakes. He'd famously come out of retirement, voluntarily turned in a star, and led West

---

[45]A few years later I'd reflect—he resembled an aged version of the pig farmer from the movie *Babe* (the glasses notwithstanding).

Point through the aftermath of a debilitating cheating scandal in the mid-1970s.

To his credit, I think General Andrew Jackson Goodpaster realized it wasn't my fault I was at the Pentagon for eight weeks.[46] He recovered from his old-school disdain and asked me how things were going at the academy.

{Whenever people get my name wrong, they seem to call me "Greg." My wife gets Jennifer in place of Stephanie, and I get Greg. Must be the four letters ending with a "g." During my internship at the Pentagon, there was a kind lieutenant colonel who showed up for his assignment one week into my stint. This lieutenant colonel started calling me Greg on his second day at the Pentagon. I didn't correct him right away, figuring he'd catch on to my actual name. He didn't. By the third day, I was in too deep. He called me Greg for the next seven weeks, and I answered dutifully. I still have a picture of the Pentagon signed by a number of people I worked with that summer. I came upon it last year during our move to the Seattle area. "Greg---thanks for all your hard work…"

I didn't think about it until writing this story, but that was a true Say Anything experience. He was a nice man, and I should have just told him my name. It's a blatant case providing more evidence of how difficult it can be to get the people you lead to Say Anything—even their own names.}

---

[46]Although I chose the assignment so I could spend more time with my fiancé that summer.

So back to mid-level officers at the Pentagon and their overall importance in the big picture. A selfless servant such as Tony Echevarria will never end up on the cover of *Time* magazine, but his expertise and thinking will inform the Secretary of Defense, the National Security Advisor, and the four-star generals of the world. It's actually monumentally important what Echevarria believes about what Clausewitz believed. How we employ our military power could result from a particular officer's philosophical stance —a stance informed by Tony's translation and interpretation.

The United States' entire military approach might pivot based on the Napoleonic-era writings of a mid-level officer (von Clausewitz) from the Prussian version of the Pentagon, interpreted by a modern-day mid-level officer turned academic expert. "A center of gravity," explains Lieutenant Colonel Echevarria in the most plain terms I could find, "is more than a critical capability; it is the point where a certain centripetal force seems to exist, something that holds everything else together."

9. POSITIVE INTENT

If someone doesn't trust you, it doesn't matter how well you measure your words, the other person will misinterpret you. If someone trusts you implicitly, it doesn't matter how poorly you phrase something, the other person will assume you meant well.
-Bruce Brown, Proactive Coaching

You have reached the centripetal point of this book: the Center of Gravity. Forging a fearless culture—one where your people share every idea and communicate candidly—turns on one thing: **positive intent**. It is what holds everything else together. If your people are going to Say Anything and everything they are thinking, wondering, or pondering, it must be for the good of the organization. This is an effect, not a capability. We are not suggesting people must be *capable* enough to have a positive impact on the organization; we are arguing that must be their *intent*. When Steven Hauschka suggests the Seahawks not kick a field goal, its requisite that he says so intending to help the team win the game. If Doug's West Point classmate advises that his unit is not prepared for the mission in Afghanistan, he must do so with no hint of personal agenda.

When a junior officer tells the captain of a submarine to do another periscope sweep...

When Doug tells his dad to lean back on corner kicks...

When someone throws out the idea of honey pots on the top of telephone poles...

When a nurse reminds, "Wash your hands..."

When Timmy replies he doesn't understand what it means to "turn your back on the ball..."

When a mother-in-law admits she doesn't want to go to Abilene...

And when Laura Lothrop suggests a display teaching people how to transplant their garden foliage...

It must all be said with positive intent. It's the Center of Gravity. And while much of what we teach as leader developers hinges on the idea "leadership is not about you," this, in fact, is all about you. As a leader, you must *create* this positive intent. You must, or none of this will work. How do you do that? How in the world do you get every single person in your organization to speak out loud with the greater good in mind? How, as a leader, can you possibly create positive intent in those you lead?

It's simple.

You assume it.

Simple, yet one of the hardest things you will ever do. If you want to lead so people speak fearlessly, you must change the way you think, permanently and resoundingly. If you change the way you think, you will change the way you lead, and you will—literally —change the intent of the people who follow you. There's overwhelming scientific proof of this.

The nonprofit organization Young Life has a stated mission of introducing kids to Jesus and helping them grow in their faith. But almost as important as that purpose is the way Young Life approaches its mission. Leaders must **earn the right to be heard.** This made sense in 1941 when Jim Rayburn founded the venture. It makes eminently more sense in an age where kids are rightly skeptical of truth, adults, and agendas. Earning the right to be heard means you set an example, listen (to anything), care, wait, and if a kid eventually wants to hear what you have to say, you share it then and then only. We hope over the first half of this book, we've earned the right to be heard. We've researched well, demonstrated expertise, shared our hearts, told stories about our kids, to arrive at this critical point. We have lived out this idea of assuming positive intent. It's changed us, benefited those we lead, and fueled our motivation to write this book. And, the aim of this book is to impact you and, in turn, those around you.

Assume positive intent.

You've probably heard that phrase before. Don't assume[47] you know what we mean by it. Because what we mean is to see the world and those you lead in an entirely different way...

> "Sir, the guys are talking. You're losing respect within the platoon, sir. We've all noticed you're spending a lot of time around the commander, over here in the headquarters. You're even sleeping over here, sir. This isn't where you should be, L-T. I really think when you bunk up tonight, you should come back and be with the platoon," Sergeant Davies _____.

What word goes in the blank? Seriously. Pick a word. Is it berated? Did Sergeant Davies berate me? Other options include: barked, scolded, rebuked, chastised, admonished, or reprimanded. Maybe he just stated, observed, or commented. With sun shining on his words, we might decide he recommended, suggested, or encouraged. There's only one soldier in that whole platoon who could have said to me that day at the National Training Center what Davies had the guts to put forth, and he's the guy who said it. But the truth of his words didn't depend on the messenger. Only my

---

[47] See what we did there?

interpretation and response rested on who delivered the bad news. How I perceived his intent was on me.

Of course Steven Hauschka wanted to win the NFC Championship game. Pete Carroll could have inferred self-doubt, weakness, selfishness, or even cowardice from Hauschka's comments. Instead, he assumed positive intent. When a nurse says "Remember to wash your hands," a doctor can assume she's on a power trip, doesn't like him, or gets off on nagging people. Or, he can assume she cares about her patients. The research we shared earlier on silence in hospitals drew a conclusion about the courageous nurses who speak up successfully: "they begin by explaining their positive intent."

Here's what we are suggesting: **Never, ever make anyone explain it**. Just assume it. As the leader, you have the power in the relationship. Don't send thousands of nurses, deck officers, field goal kickers, and assistant managers to communication training. Instead, create positive intent throughout your organization—by assuming it.

In their book *Difficult Conversations*, experts from the Harvard Negotiation Project encourage all of us to **disentangle impact from intent**. They so aptly point out we don't know what others intend. We are aware of the impact words and actions have on us, but we can never judge beyond a reasonable doubt the other person's motives. Such a hard lesson to swallow, but an invaluable one.

Larry Olson, a trusted friend and an early contributor to the wildly successful veterans organization Team Red, White, and Blue is also a publishing industry expert. He's what Adam Grant of Wharton would call a *giver,* so when we launched our Kickstarter campaign and set out to self-publish SAY ANYTHING, we reached out to Larry.[48] I sent him the introduction to the book and asked him for his feedback. Larry did not answer. I waited a few weeks and sent Larry another email. This time, I provided a link to our fundraising effort and encouraged him to share ideas on how we could improve. I also asked if he might be able to help with marketing the book. Crickets. I waited another week and crafted a final email. I told Larry I knew he was busy and had done so much for me already, but we could really use his help on this one. I asked for some recommendations. Larry did not reply.

It crossed my mind that Larry was angry. He was the driving force behind *Leadership Lessons from West Point*. He'd helped the academy's Department of Behavioral Sciences and Leadership in so many ways a decade ago. I reasoned Larry might be upset because after all he'd done for me, I was now giving a stiff-arm to traditional publishing. Or maybe I'd done something else wrong. I didn't know exactly what I'd done, but it must have been something. I drew the conclusion Larry was through with me. But I took one more shot. I sent him a text:

---

[48] Earlier in the book we referenced takers. Givers, on the contrary, are those Adam Grant says "contribute to others without expecting anything in return."

Hey Larry. Sent you a few emails but didn't hear back. So was thinking 1) you didn't like the book, 2) you're super busy as always, or 3) I did something wrong. If 1 or 2, no worries! If 3, I'm sorry. :) Anyway…latest question was whether you have any publicist recommendations. Hope all is well!

Two hours later, Larry texted back:

Hey Doug! I'm so sorry. 4) Larry has been laid off and no longer gets emails sent to lolson@****.com. After 22 years at the company and over 30 in publishing, I am now out on the job market.

Ouch. We are not aware of what's inside the other person's head. We are only aware of the impact his or her words or (in)actions have on us.

Once you've assumed positive intent, you hear things in a different way.

For me, everything I did as a leader changed on a fall day in the basement of West Point's Thayer Hall. The colleagues I taught with at the academy were easily the most talented collection of people I will ever be around. In the office to my right was Captain Chip Daniels, a Virginia Tech graduate and Duke MBA. Chip's been promoted "below the zone" three times, and is one of the youngest brigade commanders in the U.S. Army. He's also bright, of impeccable character, and a huge college football fan. Someday, Chip will cement his beliefs on Clausewitz and Center of Gravity and our nation's fate will turn on his decisions. He will be a four-star general. That's a good thing for all of us.

A few ticks counter-clockwise sat a future Dean of West Point. Lieutenant Colonel Bernie Banks was every cadet's favorite teacher. He commanded an Apache helicopter squadron in Korea, earned his PhD from Columbia, and now serves as the head of the Department of Behavioral Sciences and Leadership.

Kitty-corner from Banks sat Steve Ruth. Steve has the largest barrel chest you will ever see. He ironed all his shirts with precision. My kids remember he used to come out and play intramural softball in his service uniform. He'd swing the bat hoping his tie did not get in the way. Then he'd run to first base wearing shined, leather low-quarters. Steve had been president of his class at Texas A&M, served several tours in Iraq, and commanded the U.S. Military Academy Prep School.[49] Ruth was so proud of his Lone Star roots, he signed

---

[49]On-site at West Point.

everything (official documents and all) "SRT"—Steve Ruth from Texas. Adjacent to Ruth and Banks were Donna Brazil, Pat Michaelis, and Todd Woodruff—world-class leaders all of them.

Our eldest team member resided in an office near the front door of the bullpen. Just about every day, Dave Pursley wore a curious black cardigan none of us even realized was in the Army's wardrobe. But Dave could wear whatever he wanted. He'd enlisted and served in Special Forces for a number of years before joining the officer ranks. With a master's from Purdue, "Big Purse" moved into strategic planning when he left West Point and was yet another colleague the Army promoted ahead of schedule.

I was tucked in the space across from Dave's, with probably the most accomplished team member of all, when my leadership philosophy changed forever. Major Everett Spain grabbed the tiny, corner office on purpose. If he didn't suffer in it, someone else would. As the most junior officer in the bullpen, I felt guilty having such a nice space while Ev squeezed into a glorified closet. Everett Spain was a leader among leaders. As he sees it, leaders "eat" last.[50]

One morning Everett and I connected to discuss teacher development for next summer's cohort of incoming faculty. Ev had run the process the previous year (for Todd, Chip, Steve, Dave, and me), and I would be leading the charge in June. The Faculty

---

[50] Simon Sinek used this phrase as the title of a best-selling book. The idea has been a central artifact of military culture for decades.

Development Workshop (FDW) as we called it, was a crash-course in West Point's core leadership offering: PL300. We spent six weeks as students of every fifty-five-minute lesson we would soon teach. When August rolled around, Lieutenant Colonel Brazil and Everett handed us the conch, and each of us taught four practice lessons—on transformational leadership, culture, power and influence, or any number of topics. During the practice classes, the experienced faculty would role-play students. Some of them asked cynical questions, pretended to fall asleep, talked too long, and shuffled their books and papers prematurely—as the end of class approached. Cadets at West Point are committed and bright for the most part, but they are still college students. The experienced teachers were trying to get us ready. Everett and I were debating the merits of this role-playing tradition when he raised his voice slightly and declared, "I hate that stuff! I hate it."

Everett Spain is a real-life version of Forrest Gump (except he's the genius version). His life almost ended during U.S. Army Ranger School when hypothermia brought his heartbeat to a halt. A Blackhawk helicopter flew him to the closest emergency room, and medical personnel revived him. After his engineer company won the prestigious Draper Award as the best unit in Europe, Ev studied business at Duke and returned to West Point to teach. He became the first (and only) academy faculty member to receive a Purple Heart while serving as a teacher. During the summer of 2004, he deployed to Iraq and was struck by shrapnel. After departing his temporary teaching assignment and returning to the regular Army, Spain served as the aide de camp to General Petraeus for two years. Part of the job interview was keeping up with Petraeus on a five-mile run. Everett later worked as a White House Fellow, commanded a garrison in Germany, was promoted early to colonel, and earned his PhD at Harvard (where he won the highest peacetime medal for valor while acting as an impromptu first responder during the Boston Marathon bombing). He's now back at West Point (in a bigger office).

So there I sat in the fall of 2003, startled by Everett's proclamation that he hated the role-playing stuff. *Is this just Everett being Everett?* I thought to myself. He is simultaneously the nicest and most competitive guy on the planet. He does not lack for forceful opinions, walks at a fast pace because he always has too much to do, and will not suffer fools for more than a few days. He'd also sell all his possessions if it meant saving your house from foreclosure, has adopted a child from China (with his wife Julia), and drew cadets to his office in droves because they admired his selfless and caring professionalism. So which Ev was I talking to on this morning?

"Why, Everett? Why do you hate that stuff?"

"I hate it," he continued, "because I have never met a bad cadet. Never. We teach our new faculty they fall asleep, wield cynical tongues, and act like slackers. We set up those expectations. But I mean it, I've never met a bad one. They are all trying to do the right thing."

I don't remember when I decided to experiment with Everett Spain's view of the world. It was not right away. I left his office mocking him a bit. *Never met a bad cadet.* Yeah, whatever. But I decided to visit a few of his classes. No one slept, no one shuffled papers, and no one asked cynical questions. Everett's body language beamed respect for his students. There was vibrant, intelligent dialogue in his classrooms. I could step out of his room a few feet into the hall and look through windows into other classes. I can't say for sure, but, I might have spotted some drool. There were glazed-over looks, signs of fear, and hints of quiet desperation. And then—boom! You pop back into Everett's PL300 lesson and hands are in the air, students are debating how to best motivate Private Carter, and Everett is standing in the corner watching them thrive.

If you cringe at the spectacle of lab rats being treated like lab rats, you won't like this story. But it's an enlightening introduction to the narrative of how assuming intent creates intent. In 1966, J.R. Burnham injected some ingenuity into a developing school of research: exploring how the preconceptions of experimenters impacted the final results of an experiment. Previous studies had demonstrated—conclusively—that if lab workers believed their rats were "gifted," the animals performed better on a series of maze navigations. The supervisors provided the supposedly superior rodents more physical handling, more encouragement, and less corrective feedback. Yes, we are talking about rats, the things with tails that when not in a laboratory live in a dark alley or the sewer.

Burnham wanted to up the game. He had twenty-three experimenters put the rats through a maze exercise. About half the rats underwent a brain-cortex removal surgery. The other thirteen received a "sham" surgery, where Burnham cut into their skulls and produced a slight head wound, but did not remove the cortexes. Overwhelmingly, the best performers in the maze were the rats whose "leaders" believed their brains were fully operational—had a cortex—and whose brains in fact did have a cortex. Not surprising.

©Robert Adrian Hillman

However, if a rat's brain cortex had *not* been removed, but the experimenter believed it had, performance dropped dramatically. It decreased almost to the same level as that of the rats who *actually* had their cortex taken out. {And as you probably guessed, even if an experimenter believed its rat's brain was intact, this could not overcome the absence of a cortex.)

This experiment teaches us, in essence, as long as the people you lead have a functioning brain, assuming positive intent will yield the best results—by a landslide.

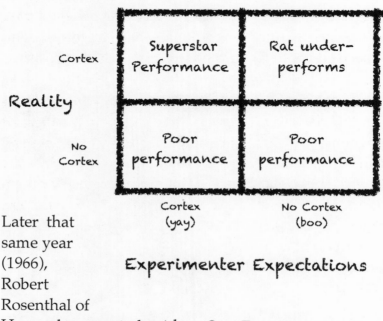

	Cortex (yay)	No Cortex (boo)
Cortex	Superstar Performance	Rat under-performs
No Cortex	Poor performance	Poor performance

Reality (left side)

Experimenter Expectations (bottom)

Later that same year (1966), Robert Rosenthal of Harvard connected with a San Francisco Bay Area educator, Lenore Jacobson. The two decided to research human subjects and determine if preconceptions about a student's learning ability would impact actual intellectual development. Their resulting work became oft-cited support for the notion of the Pygmalion Effect—the idea that our mere beliefs about others have a causal impact on their attitudes, actions, and performance.

Rosenthal and Jacobson found this to be true at the Oak Hill School. Students whose teachers had been conditioned to believe they were on the precipice of an academic burst, experienced a surge. Teachers evaluated the group as more interesting; more affectionate; more adjusted; and destined for a more successful future. However, just as researchers convinced experimenters they had the "gifted" rats (nonsense), so too were the students in the Oak Hill experiment selected randomly. The experiment at Oak Hill overwhelmingly demonstrated an impact on in-class behavior

The complexities of the research yielded some conflicting findings, but taken on the whole, the Pygmalion Effect is a scientifically validated phenomenon. Scott Snook, a retired army colonel and Harvard PhD who was instrumental in the transformation of West Point's leader development system at the turn of the century, told us, "The Pygmalion Effect is the most under-appreciated experiment in psychology, and the one with the most powerful implications for leaders."[51]

Dov Eden, a professor at Israel's Tel Aviv University, took the line of research to new heights. In 1982, Eden gained access to an Israeli Defense Forces combat command course. The IDF permitted Eden and a colleague to condition four military instructors with information similar to the lab rat experiments of the mid-1960s: a number of the command course participants were classified as *gifted*, others were

---

[51] Snook is a brilliant teacher. He now leads efforts to develop and deliver authentic leadership courses as a senior lecturer at Harvard Business School.

designated as *average*, and some were identified as *unclassifiable*. "Each instructor was then given a list of his trainees in which about a third were designated high CP, a third were unmarked to indicate regular CP, and a third were marked with a question mark indicating they were unclassifiable." Just like in 1960-something, this was complete nonsense; the designations were entirely random. The inclusion of an unclassifiable category added to the legitimacy of the ruse. Its intent was to eliminate any suspicion by the four instructors.

Seven weeks later, the results were in. The *high CP* soldiers substantially outperformed their peers. "The differences in performance evidenced a substantial Pygmalion Effect," Eden concluded, "about 15 points on a conventional 100 point grade scale." Eden drew some conclusions, which everyone on the planet who leads another human being should understand:

> The instructors were quite good leaders for those of whom they expected a lot, but not good leaders of those whom they expected less...if managers would treat all their subordinates to the same quality leadership that they lavish upon those of whom they expect the most, all would perform better.

And there you have it. Dov Eden reduced his years of research to a simple conclusion: *leaders get what they expect*—be it success in a maze, behavior in a classroom, performance in a training program, or positive contributions from their people. You create positive intent by expecting it. A bit of good news is this entire notion is made easier (although not easy) by the fact we can't know intent. We must assume it, one way or another. Be it positive or negative.

You choose.

Dov Eden is an eclectic academic. He's known as one of the world's leading authorities on the impacts of vacation time. Not a bad gig. He concocted further iterations of the IDF experiment. Turns out, he found, the Pygmalion Effect works both ways—positively and negatively. We call the negative side the Golem Effect.[52] If we believe our people are lazy, dumb, dull, or any number of negatives, we create those results. Eden also demonstrated the Pygmalion effect on a group level. In different IDF courses instructors were led to believe certain things about their entire platoon. Same results. Leaders got what they expected.

We are going to borrow a final story from Dov Eden's 1992 article in *Leadership Quarterly*. It's best delivered unedited:

> A plant manager in Israel, who had heard a lecture about expectation effects, was having a problem with the low productivity of consecutive waves of new employees. Production workers in the plant, who assembled and packaged disposable sterile medical kits for use in blood dialysis and transfusions, were native or immigrant women from Eastern Europe. In this plant, "everyone knew" that, in comparison to immigrants, natives were poor workers, adjusted slower, were

---

[52] Golem is the Hebrew word for "dumbbell."

undisciplined, took longer to reach standard production, and had difficulty maintaining it. In particular, the head production supervisor, who for years had been responsible for putting new hires to work, "knew" that the native women would give her trouble and not reach standard soon, if ever.

The plant manager believed that the native workers were as capable as the immigrants. Suspecting the operation of a Golem effect, he summoned the head production supervisor and told her that he had personally hand-picked the group of native new hires slated to come on board the following week and that they were excellent people. They should be expected to give her no problem and should attain standard production quickly. As usual she, the head supervisor, was to assume responsibility for their integration into the plant and to report any problems to him. This was followed by the smoothest intake of native new hires that anyone in the plant could remember. They achieved standard in record time and soon appreciably exceeded it. The supervisor complimented the plant manager for having improved his hiring decisions.

Everett Spain—when he told me he'd never met a bad cadet—didn't take me to a whiteboard and illustrate the fundamentals of Dov Eden's research. He didn't mention any lab rats. He wasn't trying to convince me of anything at all (other than to dispense with role-playing in our faculty development process). My friend Ev stated plainly: "I've never met a bad cadet." He believed it, and that's the key. I made a conscious decision at the outset of my second semester to never meet a bad cadet. It was an emotional time for me. I missed the first two weeks of class because my dad had died suddenly the day before our semester began.[53] I returned predestined to experience a major shift in life. It was an uphill climb. Bernie Banks, Todd Woodruff, and Chip Daniels—all amazing leaders—were my substitute teachers while I was delivering my dad's eulogy back in Washington State. Tough acts to follow. From day one, I could tell the cadets in my classes wanted those guys back. Resistance to change produces some decipherable body language. I pressed on. **I've never met a bad cadet. I've never met a bad cadet.** I felt like the little engine that could.

Eden admits there's a central element to the Pygmalion Effect research—the leaders and followers are unwitting participants. The instructors in the Israeli Defense Force experiment didn't know it was all made up. They truly believed certain soldiers in the unit had high command potential. Scott Snook put it this way: "The one thing you can do—that's totally in your power—is you can decide what to look for in those you lead." To create positive intent you truly have to believe people possess it—whether they do or not. When a fourth grade teacher believes she has a "gifted" student, everything works a bit differently. It's in the attribution the teacher makes. If the student —the student with an asterisk of excellence next to his name—fails a test, what's the teacher's assumption? *Hmmm...I must have let him down. He's too smart to fail.*

---

[53] My dad died playing golf. My enduring, final memory is of him visiting the third class I taught at West Point—a place I graduated from and later served at because of his influence.

With no asterisk, our default assumption differs. *He must not have studied. He's just not that smart. He just doesn't care.* It's the same with a comment, suggestion, or critique. We placed Bruce Brown's quote at the outset of this chapter with assurance that it's exactly where it belongs. Go look at it again. What we hear as leaders is not about the words—it's never really about the words. It comes down to how we perceived the messenger's intent.

A few days after I returned to West Point in January of 2004, a cadet arrived late to one of my morning sections. When a student shows up tardy in Thayer Hall, he has to knock on the door (calling attention to himself in front of fifteen classmates), render a salute, and announce: "Sir, Cadet Harris reports late to class." The old me would have saluted back and fired a few brain neurons wondering where the cadet had been. *He probably overslept, doesn't care about my class, and won't pay attention while he's here.* It's that fast and then I'm back to teaching before the kid even sits down. The post-Everett-Spain-me chose to process it all differently. When the cadet knocked on the door and announced he was late, I smiled at him and thought: *Must have a good reason; some other officer probably kept him late.* Just like a lab rat senses the mindset of its instructor, a person senses the lens through which his leader sees him. The thoughts that run through a leader's head have a causal impact on the people being led—influencing the way they behave and perform.[54]

For the next four and a half years, my students were great. Seriously. Every single one of them. The cadets hadn't changed. I had. I even got a little countercultural. I told my students not to knock on the door when they were late. "I know you have a good reason. Just come in and sit down." Did I truly know they had a good reason? No. But I never worried about it. I assumed they did. Maybe some of them got over on me occasionally, but it was worth it. The incredibly positive upside of thinking this way paid enormous dividends. The longer I lived out my leadership believing I'd never meet a bad cadet, the more real it became. My classes started to look less like summer practice sessions and more like Everett Spain's. And I can tell you this: the cadets returned the trust. They didn't want to let me down. To be sure, I'm not touting my own prowess as a leader. I'm simply explaining that when I changed the way I thought, everything around me changed with it. Everything. If your people are going to Say Anything —if you plan to reap the incredible benefits of everyone you lead speaking fearlessly—you must never again meet a "bad cadet." Assuming (and thus creating) positive intent is the Center of Gravity and the only path to making all this work. And it will work—anywhere—even in a medium security prison…

---

[54] Later in the book we will meet acclaimed horse whisperer Grant Golliher. He makes this same point about horses—they sense whether their trainers like them, and respond in kind.

On a warm August day, I stepped out of my black Honda Accord. As soon as my left foot hit the pavement, I whispered a short prayer: "Lord, help me to never meet a bad prisoner." I'd taken this part-time job while writing a previous book—partly to pay the bills and partly because I have a heart for the downtrodden. In my earlier teaching experiences, I'd been able to shift my mindset to one where every student I'd encountered was a good one. I took this view of others to my role at Amazon.com. I was now coaching basketball this way as well. But gazing through a chain-link fence adorned atop with barbed wire, I thought I might need a bit of divine intervention to assume positive intent inside the confines of Coyote Ridge Correctional Center.

The lock button on my remote car key triggered two sharp beeps. I slung a backpack over my shoulder and headed for the entrance to the prison. Everything about getting to my classroom would remind me these guys were *bad*. There were the uniformed guards, metal detectors, ID checks, and powerful electronic doors which slid ominously opened and closed. I placed my keys, phone, and wallet into a locker in the bathroom as instructed. Those items were not permitted on the "inside."

Once through the maze of doors and fences, I emerged into an open prison yard. To my right was the solitary confinement structure. Honestly, I'm not even sure it got as serious as solitary in a medium-security facility, but that place to the right didn't look fun. It's where you went for detention. When I reached the yard, I hesitated for a brief moment. Do I really just walk through here by myself? There were a couple "offenders" a hundred yards to my front, walking a medium-sized dog. Another goateed and tattooed man in drab clothing came at me pushing some sort of cart. I diligently moved on, picked up my pace, and headed for the education building. I had no idea what to expect from my classes; I didn't know if these guys were in for shoplifting or selling drugs. I imagined there might be an emergency button I pushed if one of them wasn't happy with a recent test grade. For a moment, I envisioned myself knifed and bleeding out on the floor, but then quickly collected my mental composure and opened up the door.

My first class was better, and worse, than I imagined. The better part was everything seemed pretty community-college-ish from an academic perspective. There was a lab full of computers, a whiteboard in every classroom, and the course enrollments were manageable at about twenty. It was worse in that I found out quickly these guys ran the gamut from murder-one to armed robbery to extortion and drunk driving. I knew my thoughts would drive my actions, and ultimately create either a Pygmalion or Golem Effect—one or the other. On paper, this was my toughest positive intent test yet.

I taught for two hours and then spent lunchtime in the secured faculty area. There was limited Internet access. I tried Facebook and espn.com but received a rejection message courtesy of the Washington State Department of Corrections. I picked up a book to read, but as I began, I was distracted by the conversations of the faculty members around me. I'm guessing it's difficult to go to work at Coyote Ridge Correctional Center every single day and maintain a positive view of these guys. I had the benefit of being there just fifteen hours per week. But the things I overheard were often difficult to stomach. It was all negative, all the time. I don't remember specific dialogue, but I remember how I felt after listening. I tried to tune it out and never meet a bad prisoner.

Nate Corbray, Daniel Shea, Nick Bunn, Silas Robbins, and Jermal Joe—these were the guys I met at Coyote Ridge. Two others also stood out as the semester went on. One of them, Percy Levy, was born in a prison—literally. His mom was locked up in a New Mexico correctional facility during his conception (apparently conjugal visits are real things), his birth, and every single year of his life. They released her when Percy was ten. *Finally*, he thought, *I get the chance to have a mom like everyone else.* Except Percy's mom wasn't like everyone else's. Not but a few days after she picked up little Percy from his twenty-third foster home, she beat the hell out of him. That became habit. The woman who gave birth to Percy—the one who was supposed to read him Dr. Seuss and make him peanut butter and jelly—instead used kitchen knives to stab him in the arm. "I'd describe the things that were done to me when I was younger," I heard Percy preach a few years later at his graduation, "but they are so brutal it's best I leave them to your imagination. That being said, your imagination will never do them justice."

Percy earned an A+ in speech class. Yet no one in the world had ever believed in Percy Levy. No one. Not a single person on this planet of seven billion had ever heard a word come out his mouth and assumed he was coating it with some sort of positive intent. The "joke" below was part of a training program both Matt and I attended in preparation to teach at Coyote Ridge—an annual requirement for everyone who works in the Washington State DOC. [55]

Q: How do you know if a prisoner is lying?
A: His lips are moving.

Put another way, every year, the DOC reminds every employee all these guys do is lie—all the time. We also "learned" prisoners are always trying to manipulate you, and to be on the defensive. I'm pretty sure these weren't official parts of the curriculum, but culture is never about what's official.

To be sure, Percy Levy had a chip on his shoulder the size of a ball and chain. He was a cynical, large, angry black man who liked to glare at people.[56] But Percy Levy was (and is) also something else—utterly brilliant.

David Walker is white, bald, slender, and not quite as angry as Percy. From what I understand, Percy

---

[55] A requirement I successfully blew off for the next two years.

[56] I'm trying to paint an authentic picture for you—if you want me to pretend I didn't notice his skin color, then please put down the book and turn on an episode of *Shark Tank*.

committed some armed robberies and left a few people badly beaten. David Walker sold drugs too many times. He sold drugs so he could buy drugs. "I was a junkie," Dave told me when he served as a teaching assistant during my third year at Coyote Ridge. "Finally my counselor had enough. I remember standing there in court and she tells the judge, 'Mr. Walker has hit bottom, furnished it, moved in, and is living there comfortably.'"

Three-strikes-and-you're-out landed David Walker a double-digit sentence. He's had plenty of time to make meaning of his life story:

I remember when I was 19. I was working the graveyard shift at a meat-cutting factory. Guys would get off work and take me to bars—drinking, getting high, and doing cocaine. One morning I wake up and I'm late for something. I go running through the kitchen past my dad. He almost never talked to me. He wasn't even there for the first nine years of my life. All the sudden on Valentine's Day in 1973 he shows up and proposes to my mom. I really didn't know what to think of him. But he grabs me in the kitchen this day and spins me around a bit. He points at me and snickers with disgust, "When you are forty, you are going to wake up alone and with nothing."

On his 40th birthday, Dave Walker woke up alone and with nothing...locked behind thick metal bars in a cold room on a prison bed. His dad's words bounced back and forth like a pinball game inside his head. He has flashbulb memory of that moment in the kitchen. David can see himself spinning around and catching the disapproving gaze of his father. The short scene kept replaying in his mind that birthday morning and he simply started to cry. Two years later, Dave Walker stood at his mother's funeral in shackles and an orange jumpsuit. His dad passed a year before that, but he didn't bother to attend the service.

After teaching at the facility for nearly three years, I can say with every ounce of sincerity: "I never met a bad prisoner." What changed me as a leader at West Point carried over to teaching in prison. The final class I taught at Coyote Ridge was an honors course in leadership. Matt and I developed it as a way to give the best inmates something positive in their lives. We limited attendance to fifteen. In order to gain a spot in the class, you needed a GPA above 3.5, could have no disciplinary infractions during the previous 365 days, and you had to write a one-page essay explaining why you belonged in the course. Over one-hundred men applied. Being tabbed the "best of the best"—for the first time in their lives—had limitless power. Men cried. We spent a ten-week quarter with these guys. There were guest speakers, leadership philosophy papers, and some of the best dialogue we'd ever experienced in a classroom. Percy and David were two of the standout students.

Percy also said a few harsh things in class. Every time he released anger, though, I assumed it came from a good place (maybe a desire to be understood). I still talk to Percy via an email system called JPay, and his wife is my Facebook friend. He's earned more privileges via good behavior and since finishing his community college program with honors, he's published four fiction books. They are urban tales, salty and real. He's actually told me a couple times not to read them. Despite the bond we formed, there's still a part of Percy that fears my judgment. You, however, can find his books on Amazon right now. Seriously. Just search for Percy Levy.[57]

Dave Walker earned his associates degree and is only a few credits away from finishing a bachelor's at Ohio University. He's done it all via snail mail. David is one of my favorite people on the planet. When he writes me these days, he talks about friend-type stuff. He's intelligent, warm, and giving. We plan to hire him. He will be a super leader developer. I want to share a few sentences of a letter Dave wrote at the conclusion of the honors leadership course. This is in no way meant to be boastful, but rather a testament to the power of assuming positive intent:

"I can't say with certainty what it was you said to me the morning before I graduated. After the first few words I used a great deal of my concentration to fight back the impending tears. What I did hear (yet not so much in words) was that you **believed in me**, and I can't remember a moment when I was any prouder—a moment where my life made more sense."

---

[57] *Slave to the Trade* series, and *Urban Love* series.

The note conveys two key things: 1) David is eloquent and smart, and 2) David is different because someone believed in him.

In addition to his college work, I told him to read *Primal Leadership, Multipliers, Difficult Conversations,* and Edgar Schein's *Organizational Culture and Leadership.*[58] He read them all and sent a mini-report on each. Along with one of his reports, he sent another letter. David Walker was speaking fearlessly —discussing his post-confinement plans and suggesting he could become a world-class leader developer (with an amazing backstory).

Power, past experience, or fear of judgment could all get in the way of a dream that big. David spoke it. It's our job as leaders to dignify the try and empower those we lead to say what's on their minds and in their hearts. Release the people you lead from the burden of saying things the right way.

Even inside a medium-security prison, assuming positive intent worked to create positive intent. A group of armed robbers, murderers, and drug dealers moved past the muzzles that had been part of their required dress code—and started to Say Anything. We could have taken our honors leadership course participants, put them in khakis and button-downs, and plopped them in a section at Harvard Business School. No one would have known the difference.

---

[58] All outstanding books relating to leadership and leader development. See our recommended reading list at the end.

I should have known all this already—before Everett Spain ever told me, or I witnessed Scott Snook teach, or read Dov Eden's research. I sat in a different place at West Point in early May of 1991—not Everett's small office, but an enormous auditorium named after one of the academy's alumni: General Dwight Eisenhower. "Stormin'" Norman Schwarzkopf had returned from Iraq and scheduled a visit to his alma mater. Before all four thousand of us gathered in "Ike Hall" to hear the general, we celebrated the Gulf War victory with a parade on the military academy's picturesque plain. I remember three things: it was incredibly hot and humid (exacerbated by our thick wool uniforms), a cadet somewhere to my left front passed out while we stood in formation, and the West Point band played an instrumental version of Bette Midler's "Wind Beneath My Wings" as the burly and masculine Schwarzkopf rode slowly by the Corps of Cadets perched on the back of an army jeep. Later that evening, General Schwarzkopf went a bit off script as something raised his ire:[59]

> You're leading people; you are leading human beings. I've seen competent leaders who stood in front of a platoon, and saw it as a platoon. But I've seen great leaders who stood in front of a platoon and saw it as forty-four individuals—each of whom has their hopes; each of whom has their dreams; each of whom

---

[59] This is a somewhat deceptive turn of phrase as Schwarzkopf had no actual script. But it was a detour from his topic: competence and character.

wants to do good. People don't join the military to do poorly. Nobody goes downtown and says, "Gee, I think I'll enlist in the army so I can screw up." They don't do that. They say, "I think I'll enlist in the army because I want to do better." And if they fail, their leader fails.

Later that night, after the speech had concluded, a faculty member asked Schwarzkopf where the impassioned middle portion of his address came from. What inspired the tangent? "You know," General Schwarzkopf spewed with righteous indignation, "we sit around in our offices on Friday afternoon and talk—laugh even—about all the things our soldiers screwed up that week. 'Can you believe what Joe did?' And I hate that; it drives me crazy. Our men and women want to do good."

This assumption of positive intent is the Center of Gravity—the thing that holds everything else together. If I were building a leader, I'd first give her integrity, and then I'd equip her with this perspective on others. Before you read any further, stop for a moment and ponder: what's your own mindset about the intent and motivation of those you lead? What do you choose to believe?

THE TOOLS

The United States Army brought a simple but powerful leadership model out of the 1980s:

Be, Know, Do

The model has been translated into a business book and studied by some of the world's best for-profit and nonprofit organizations. SAY ANYTHING is littered with the **be.** In so many ways (including mindset shift), the ideas within go straight to **who** you are as a leader. We've also established the case in the form of **know**ledge: the problem, the dynamics, and the groundwork. The last third of SAY ANYTHING is all **do**. How do leaders—in a practical sense—inspire ideas, cultivate candor, and forge fearless cultures? You do it, in part, by proving it's safe, dignifying every try, and being genuinely curious. Those are the tools that will forge and sustain cultures of fearless communication.

10. PROVE IT'S SAFE

Shoes, sir; the men need shoes, Colonel.
-Mr. Rawlins in the movie *Glory*

During my final two years teaching at West Point, I served as advisor and speechwriter for the Dean of Academics. Because of the odd symmetry of the Dean's 19th century office, I lucked into a huge corner space overlooking the Hudson River. I did some memorable things serving in that role. We once visited Kiefer Sutherland on the set of the TV series *24*. It was an eclectic job. When not on Hollywood sets, I scripted speeches, provided input on the academy's academic program, and got really good at PowerPoint. During the fall of my first year on the job, I wrote, printed, and organized the Dean's talk at an awards ceremony. But when we arrived at the venue, I discovered I'd misplaced the final page. The speech came up four lines short.

The general didn't get mad about stuff like this. I deserved some harsh words or sideways glances, but he remained calm. While we waited backstage, I emailed the Dean's executive assistant and asked him to send the speech. Within a minute, the text filled my Blackberry. I showed the final lines to my boss, who read them as he walked toward the stage. He returned the Blackberry just as he passed through the curtains. After sitting on the stage for the next half hour, he stepped to the podium. He read several minutes of material, and when he came upon the last four lines—the ones I'd left on my desk—he didn't miss a beat. I scrolled the email on my phone as my boss recited the lines *verbatim*. He'd memorized the words in under sixty seconds, held them in his head while sitting on stage for the length of a sitcom, and then delivered them seamlessly at the end of the talk. Wow. When we gathered to leave, he patted me on the back, and in an almost celebratory tone exclaimed, "We got it done." Um, yeah. "We" did, sir. I forgot the last page, and "we" got it done.

The Dean was super smart—a genius even. He also led from the heart. One random evening I got an idea to surprise my oldest son, John, with a trip to Boston. I asked for a last-minute day off. He was the kind of guy who didn't even blink: "Great idea. Have a wonderful time." Hands-down, he was the most incredible person you could ever ask to serve. The general was caring, approachable, and humble. He downplayed his own power and grew angry only when presented with reports of injustice or dishonesty. And that's why it's so perplexing that I still silenced my rightful concerns.

The autumn of my first year working for the Dean, a prominent sports figure offered him tickets to the World Series. The gesture clearly violated the government's prohibition against gifts based on "official position."[60] The U.S. Office of Government Ethics limits the value of such gifts to twenty dollars (which in this day and age might be a pen and a fancy bookmark). These tickets were worth about a

---

[60] Such as being the Dean of the United States Military Academy or even his speechwriter.

thousand dollars more than twenty dollars. My boss had spent his entire career as an Army lawyer. He was one of the best. For decades, he'd found ways for commanders to say "Yes" to common sense and "No" to bureaucracy and legalism. He was also a little kid inside, and these tickets were a dream come true. I'm not sure he ever fully considered the implications. But accepting them was not within ethical guidelines. There was no gray area.

My boss proved exceedingly honest during the years I worked for him. It was not his power or my past experience that kept me mum in this instance; it was fear of disapproval.[61] I didn't want him to feel I had questioned his integrity. So I said nothing. I hinted in the way co-pilots do, tried to find a reason we couldn't go, and asked several people for advice. I didn't *do* nothing, but I *said* nothing.

As a last resort, I spoke to head legal counsel at the academy. I queried whether accepting the tickets was unethical. I knew the answer before I ever called her, but I called her anyway. She encouraged me to do the right thing and speak up, but assured me our conversation was confidential. To this day, I still don't know what would have happened if I'd just marched in to the Dean's office and pronounced: "Sir, we cannot take these tickets!" He might have said, "You're right. Thanks for calling that out."

I found a way for us to attend the event legally through a roundabout solution, but I never spoke up in an unmitigated way. I reflected on this experience

---

[61] Silence stemming from the fear of delivering bad news has actually been labeled the *Mum Effect* by social scientists.

often during the two years Matt and I researched the Say Anything concept. How can we possibly pull this off—this cultivating candor thing? I trusted the Dean with all my heart, but his caring leadership still couldn't get me to overcome my fear and speak up about some sports tickets. He didn't know it at the time (as we probably don't know what our people are holding back right now), but despite all his trust-building efforts, I held out when it might have mattered most.

There's one thing the Dean could have done differently though. He was the furthest thing from a power-wielding dictator, but he still could have taken step one to prove it's safe.[62] He could have told me explicitly:

"You can Say Anything to me. Anything. Anytime."

This type of categorical proclamation proved essential for Seattle's WADOT Capital as it carefully navigated the post-real-estate-bubble landscape. The company operates in a niche market, providing private funding for potential property owners. The products are like a mortgage, but on the back end WADOT receives its capital from individual investors rather than banks. Relationships with these investors —who receive a return directly from WADOT—has

---

[62] I am in no way blaming the Dean for my failure to speak up. But I'm usually candid, and I trusted him immensely. If thoughts go unsaid under those circumstances, people must be hiding in the shadows of more intense circumstances.

proven a key success factor for the company; through the mid-2000s, the small business found itself making payments to its investors even though borrowers weren't paying off their loans. Now on the downhill side of that crisis, WADOT is attempting to recruit and retain high-quality talent and implement a higher-end strategy. However, the nuances of their loan origination processes make recruiting, hiring, and developing talent difficult. "We have to find top-notch, driven employees who are are comfortable asking questions and making mistakes," explained Nicole House, WADOT's vice president. "We spend a lot of time helping people learn our processes. As we do so, I'm constantly asking them 'How's it going for you? Am I handling things okay as your leader?'" If Nicole doesn't establish this sort of open rapport, her employees won't ask and won't share their thoughts. They'll hide. And the asking-of-questions is essential.

"We had one woman (Anne) who came to us after she was surprisingly let go from her job at a traditional bank. She was naturally hard on herself and didn't want to make mistakes." All the dynamics were in place to push Anne into silent compliance: she felt judged—by herself and others; she was reeling from the stinging bite of losing her previous job; and she reported directly to Nicole— the "powerful" vice president of one of the region's fastest-growing companies. But Anne would need to ask a lot of questions as she learned WADOT's business. It was incumbent upon Nicole to prove—daily—she wanted to hear each and every inquiry.

"She felt like if she had to ask questions, it meant she was doing a poor job," House observed. "in her previous job, she managed a type of underwriting where there were checklists. That enabled her to achieve 100% accuracy." But WADOT was different. Each situation was case-by-case. Anne didn't have the assurance a rote system provided. The not-knowing made her feel inadequate. Anne's is a natural way of thinking for many high achievers. But admitting she didn't know, and asking Nicole questions was what would help her excel and was exactly what WADOT needed. So Nicole House made it crystal clear. Ask me. Anytime. All the time.

It's working. Anne has been a tremendous success, and is thriving in an environment of ambiguity and customization. Without the questions, mistakes, learning, and atmosphere of fearless inquiry Nicole House provided, WADOT would experience debilitating turnover, critical errors, and silent suffering from the likes of Anne. It's the specific direction to ask questions without fear of judgment that has made the difference.

Make your appreciation for candor explicit to those you lead. Don't assume they know you value it. Don't assume they know it's okay not to know. Say it. Say it tomorrow—even if you're not quite sure you believe in it yet. And once you've made the statement, follow it up with every fiber of who you are and how you behave. We watched a senior vice president of human resources tell her team she expected them to speak freely; she wanted to hear all their thoughts. Weeks would go by, and she would re-state the expectation, but no one spoke up. Leah finally sought out the counsel of a trusted friend. "I just don't get it. I'm telling them I want to hear their thoughts, but no one will share."

"When you're asking someone to give her point of view," the friend inquired, "what does your body language say?"

Our expressions of power muzzle our people. We must make ourselves smaller in stature if we expect to hear it all. When a technology server crashes and you need the team to act quickly, stand in front of the room and command the situation. But when you're breaking down performance from the previous quarter and asking for input on how the team can do better, choose a seat near the middle of the circle, hunch over a bit, and smile. *You must skillfully toggle between directing the group in moments of execution and becoming just another member of the team in moments of learning and discovery.*

Remi Hajjar—another stellar leader whom I taught with at West Point—was a master at facilitating discussions. Sometimes we would tape our classes as a learning exercise to improve our teaching. Remi always made me better. He showed me one time how class participation dropped when I stood in front of the room. It would pick up drastically when I took a seat among the students. Such a simple shift in the power dynamic—subjugating my position of authority—encouraged people to speak up.

Leah—the aforementioned senior vice president— eventually "moved on to other opportunities." She asked and asked for input, but her domineering presence (in combination with other behaviors) prevented people from trusting her sincerity. She also held tightly her power, constantly angling within the organization to gain a political upper-hand. Her people saw it, and all they could think about around Leah was saving face. Ultimately, it weakened team performance and cost her a job.

Making it loud and clear—both verbally and non-verbally—is simply the first step. You will inevitably have to do much more. If you're leading the gentleman we mentioned earlier—the one whose boss told him to seek help if he struggled with the marketing project and then belittled him when he asked—your words will ring hollow. Your direct proclamation may even kindle cynicism inside those who've heard it all before. You must start by telling them it's safe—that they can Say Anything—and then you will have to prove it's safe to all those who have been burned in the past or just don't believe.

The most compelling way to demonstrate that the waters of candor are safe is to dive in yourself. When you are the formal leader—the person with the legitimate power—you forge fearlessness in others when you demonstrate your humanity and speak vulnerably.

James Cameron spent five years building Walmart's Leadership Academy before the company promoted him to vice president and asked him to tackle global optimization of all its leader development.[63] Cameron grew up a bit of a rebel. He got kicked out of school

---

[63] Not *that* James Cameron (of *Titanic* and *Avatar* fame).

when he was sixteen. He never attended college. And as a young lieutenant in the British army, he almost earned a court-martial for driving his car across a military post at reckless speeds. He's no fan of pomp, and thus no fan of the Royal Family concept, but he'll occasionally mention meeting the Queen to receive his Commander of the British Empire award.[64] James did some brilliant work as the head of counter-terrorism for the U.K. He understands global issues and politics as well as anyone on the planet. When he speaks about Middle Eastern conflict, dictators in Latin America, or extremism in Eastern Europe, executives at Walmart soak it all up—appreciating the chance to further their understanding of an increasingly global economy.

James sometimes goes out of his way to sound smart. He has a sharp wit, a short temper, and a small corner in his heart reserved for his insecurities. Never did his team trust him more than when he pulled up a chair in a small circle and admitted, "I think I'm as smart as anyone. But I live in constant fear of people's judgment because I don't have a college degree. I compensate for it quite a bit actually, and it can get in my way. It's something I really need to overcome." The team later watched James admit this to a group of forty aspiring company vice presidents. Those were deep, dark waters James jumped into with that admission.

©Gino Crescoli

---

[64] CBE: one rung below knighthood.

According to Geoff Webb, one of James's direct reports, "We never trusted him more or felt closer to him than when he shared that part of himself."

Scotty Smiley, the U.S. Army's first active-duty blind officer, lost both his eyes in Iraq when an unshaven man in a gray Opel blew himself up just thirty yards in front of Smiley's vehicle. After months of recovery, Scotty climbed Mount Rainier, surfed in Hawaii, and jumped out of an airplane. He went on to earn his MBA at Duke and returned to his alma mater—West Point—to teach leadership. At the outset of all his classes (and now all his public appearances) Scotty would inform the students: "You can raise your hand. But I can't see. So your hand will probably be in the air for a really long time." It's not Scotty's power which will prevent people from speaking up; it's the uncertainty of a rare situation. *What do I do with this blind teacher?* Smiley recognizes this and makes fun of himself. He publicizes his vulnerability—even when it's obvious to everyone around him—in order to connect with people and put them at ease.[65]

If you want to see an entertaining and impressive display of vulnerability, watch Conan O'Brien's graduation speech to the Dartmouth Class of 2011. He delivered the address not long after being fired as host of *The Tonight Show*—his dream job.[66]

---

[65]It's not always obvious to people Smiley is blind. You can read his entire, amazing story in the book *Hope Unseen: The Story of the U.S. Army's First Blind Active-Duty Officer* (co-authored by Doug).

[66] The speech is easily accessible on YouTube.

> There are few things more liberating in this life than having your worst fear realized.
> —Conan O'Brien

There are also few things more liberating to your people than having their leader share his or her worst fear, biggest mistake, or even just a word of apology, admission, or uncertainty. Vulnerability begets trust. Make yourself vulnerable—and prove it's safe for others to speak fearlessly in your direction—through what you're willing to say and the attitude of humility with which you say it. Amy Edmondson, an aforementioned professor and expert on the topic of leader-follower communication, backs up this idea:

> Leaders must facilitate vital interpersonal exchanges by creating a climate of psychological safety in which it's expected people will speak up and disagree. A basic way to create such a climate is to model the behaviors: acknowledging ignorance about a topic or area of expertise, and conveying awareness of one's own fallibility.

Get everyone on board with the idea divergence of thought is a virtue—agreement that disagreement is a good thing when done with positive intent. Inspire this perspective by being vulnerable enough that others trust you. No one on James Cameron's team cared that his resume lacked a college degree. His substantial intellect was self-evident. But every one of them expressed heightened regard for James upon hearing his courageous admission. They knew—in that moment—their boss was willing to Say Anything to them, and they began to believe reciprocation would prove safe.

You've **told them** explicitly...

You're **sitting in the middle** of meetings as opposed to at the head of the table...

You've worked on establishing **welcoming body language**...

You're even saying you're sorry, occasionally **admitting you don't know**, and opening up a bit...

Yet many of your people **still aren't sure** it's safe.

There's one final step you can take: **rope off a small boundary area**.

An allegory came out of the latter half of last century which we've seen referred to several times as the product of a "social science study." However, we've been strongly committed to solid research throughout this book and admit openly we could find no actual academic support for what we're about to share. But it paints a nice picture of a story we will tell about a friend named Seth.

In the 1970s, social psychologists suggested educational practices were suffocating young learners. Experts looked inside and outside the classroom for ways to provide children freedom and room to discover. One experiment involved recess. A school district volunteered to test a fence-free playground. Researchers theorized taking the fence down would encourage children to wander farther from the swing sets and slides to explore new turf. So they selected a school and removed the fence. Before the boundary came down, kids spent recess at the edges of the area. Certainly some would stay close to the jungle gyms at the center of the playground, but others stood near the fence corners and made up new handshakes.

When the fence was removed for the experiment, behavior changed significantly, but not as expected. The kids who had skirted the boundary no longer had any idea where they could venture and still be "safe." All the kids *retreated* to the center of the playground area. Although surprising, the results were profound nonetheless: **the fence made it safe and actually enhanced risk-taking**.

One of the first people we spoke to about this Say Anything idea was a friend named Seth. At the time, Seth was a fairly new high school ministry director at a large suburban church. He'd asked for advice on getting people to open up at team meetings. He was an energetic and bold leader—possibly hampered by his own small doses of sarcasm and a dry wit. Like most people who take on a new role, Seth had lots of ideas. The team, however, liked the status quo. Sometimes they would all just look at him when he asked for input at team meetings.

©Leszek Glasner

As we talked more, Seth revealed one thing he just didn't want to hear: members of his team compare him to his predecessor. He didn't want to hear input prefaced with: "Well the way Ike used to do it was…" So we recommended Seth put up a fence. Let those you lead know it's not a good idea to go over "there," but the team is free to venture absolutely anywhere else. Seth had a sincere desire to hear his people speak fearlessly. He wanted to hear everything (with one exception). What a perfect opportunity to prove it's safe:

Make it explicit: I want to hear everything you have to say. Speak fearlessly...

Jump in yourself: I'm insecure, I admit, about how good Ike was at this job. He's a hard act to follow.

Rope off a boundary: So I really do want to hear anything and everything, with one exception: please don't tell me how Ike used to do it. Other than that, Say Anything.

When you do this effectively—and people start to trust—be ready to assume positive intent because you will hear things that sting. It's excruciating emotional work at times. You must assume positive intent, and then you must lead. Listening to the most candid thoughts of your people—and thanking them for their input—requires true belief in the call of leadership. These commitments to the hard work of serving others will distinguish the person (leader) from the title (boss). In writing this book, we've received some strikingly candid feedback:

"Some of your stories look like you're puffing your own chest as a leader."[67]

---

[67] Not our intent of course, and we tried to edit accordingly.

"I didn't get at all where you were going with that story…you lost me and I had a hard time coming back."

"Not at all the right place for humor."

When the candid thoughts start to pour in, the unfiltered words of those you lead will challenge your heart and mind. We must prove to those we lead that ideas will not be mocked, candor will not incur wrath, and it's safe to jump into the water. These steps we've shared are merely building blocks. You must start here, then be excited when someone makes the slightest comment or shares even an odd, unsolicited idea. You must celebrate every toe in the water…

11. DIGNIFY EVERY TRY

*Great spirits have always
experienced violent opposition
from mediocre minds.*
-Albert Einstein

Horses can really dig. Your average, unbroken colt or filly will carve a four-foot hole into the middle of a polo field during the time it takes its owner to eat a ham sandwich and drink a glass of lemonade. Some horses, the ones with hooves made of jackhammer, will even dig through concrete. Grant Golliher's boss didn't like digging. He'd invested a ton of money into grooming the landscape at Calypso Quarter Horses. It was a nice place. Grant was expected to keep it nice.

The ranch—a gorgeous spot of the world just south of Sun Valley, Idaho—had been beautifully sculpted with a brown, wooden show barn as its focal point. To the backside of the barn, the Wood River ran serenely through one of the property's lush, green pastures. To the barn's front was a sturdy hitching rail with a gravel surface below it. Log fences–which matched the pine-like color and knotty structure of the hitching rail—traced the internal and external borders of Calypso. The ranch was manicured yet functionally practical. Horses could drop manure at their leisure, but you would never know it from looking around. There were no droppings anywhere. Boss's orders meant the manure was picked up about as quickly as it had been deposited. It was a real, working ranch, but they kept it pristine.

dignify: make something seem worthy and impressive

Red—a chestnut-colored colt who Grant had purchased with his own money and brought along for his summer on the ranch—threatened the beautiful surroundings. He was an enthusiastic digger. Calypso Quarter Horses did not welcome digging. To make matters worse, Grant was the working pro for the ranch's Bellevue Polo Club, responsible for training the horses-in-residence. He couldn't have his own animal pawing through the dirt and leaving spots of unearthed soil all around. His credibility as a trainer would suffer, and the boss would have his neck.

Golliher's dissatisfaction with his horse slowly churned into anger. Not only did he have to fill in the hole every time Red dug one up, but the horse made him look bad. His frustration peaked one day when Red dug a deep hole in the gravel right in front of the main barn—the ranch's focal point. He'd tied the horse to the hitching rail, and while inside the Polo Club building, Red spooned out a two-foot pile of dirt. *By golly*, he thought, gritting his teeth, *I'm going to break you of this digging thing. I'm going to teach you a lesson.* So he led Red away from the hitching post and along the right side of the barn. About fifty feet diagonal from the back corner of the brown building, he tethered him to a cottonwood tree about as wide around as a fire hydrant. Grant intended to isolate Red—to make him stand by himself like a school kid would sit in the corner of a classroom.

The best way to break a horse of a digging habit was to restrain his feet. Having placed Red out there by himself, tied to that tree, Grant then hobbled the horse's two front feet together so he couldn't move. He did take one precaution; he intentionally tied Red to a tree surrounded by dirt. That way, if Red fell, the dirt would soften the blow. With Red hobbled and tethered behind the barn, Grant headed out to lunch with a couple friends.

Training horses had been Grant Golliher's life right from the start. Growing up in Wyoming, he learned from his father; his dad gave him the chance to break nearly every one of the family mules. "Show 'em who's boss," his dad would say. "Don't give 'em a choice." If a mule refused to listen, punishment of all varieties ensued. Grant had seen guys take a club as thick as a stovepipe and literally beat a horse into submission. **Once it was scared to death, the horse would stop moving and do what you told him.** Some horses caught on quickly and had only to endure a bit of pain and punishment. Others fought and fought—and forced the horseman to get creative. From Wyoming to Texas to Idaho, that was how they trained horses. The Grants of the world took away their freedom to choose the wrong thing.

When Grant returned from lunch that day, he expected to find Red had learned his lesson—or at least understood he meant business. Red was a good horse—a great polo prospect with long-term value. But Grant had to cure his one bad habit. There would be no more digging at the hitching rail. Grant made a left turn around the right side of the barn and walked toward the cottonwood tree. From about fifty feet, it appeared Red was lying on the ground. Grant picked up his pace and trotted toward the horse.

Sure enough, Red occupied an awkward position beneath the tree. He was lying in the dirt with a broken neck. His body was on its side. His feet were out sideways, and his head dangled in the air with a rope around it. That horse had been a free spirit. He wanted to dig, hobbled or not. So Red probably dug despite the restraints. During the digging, he tripped and fell to the ground. But because Grant had tied his legs to each other, he couldn't get back up. His lifeless eyes stared blankly into his trainer's. Red had trusted Grant. He hadn't fought when Grant led him to the tree. He hadn't fought when Grant tied him up. He'd only struggled a bit when Grant restrained his feet.

Grant Golliher imagined Red falling, trying to breathe as the rope strangled him. Red probably panicked. He undoubtedly kicked his legs aimlessly in a struggle to regain his footing. That rope suffocated Red—choked his life away—in the time it took his trainer to eat a ham sandwich and drink some lemonade. Grant's stomach went sick. He untied the rope from the tree and lowered Red's limp head to the ground. He'd cured Red of his digging.

Grant was the boss. Grant Golliher wasn't a mean person. He loved horses. But this is how he had been taught. Tethering and hobbling was standard procedure. He shouldn't have left Red there by himself, but it never crossed his mind the horse would fall and suffocate.

Traditional horse training culture blamed the animal. Grant had grown up hearing his peers talk about that "sorry S.O.B." "He was just a bad-minded horse," they would grumble. **The trainers made the horses the scapegoats for their own failures.** The horses that conformed to the demands—they were the good horses. They fit in. Grant and his peers treated the ones that wouldn't fit in—that didn't want to have their legs tied together—as if they were stupid or evil. The humans expected the horses to fit *their* program.

Red's death humbled Grant. He wanted to be a great horseman. Red's lifeless eyes broke Grant's heart and told him he had a lot left to learn. But if he wanted to learn, he had to escape from the mindset that blamed the horse. The mules Grant had ridden as a child complied, but he could always sense the fear. Their fear made him insecure. He worried they would race off and leave him if something bad happened: if lightning struck, or a mine exploded, or rain began to pour. It was a tenuous relationship—one based on fear and submission. It was no way to lead. Red's death brought forth a pivotal moment in Grant's life. He began to see himself as the problem; the methods as the problem; his mindset as the problem. Red's death was Grant's fault. He could do things better— not only better, but right.

He decided there had to be another way. He
wanted to lead the horses,
not just rule them.

Grant took this "bounce moment" and sought out
the mentorship of the world's original horse
whisperer.[68] Tom Dorrance pioneered positive intent-
based horse training. Horses were good; wild, but
good. All the coercion and punishment and force
turned them into agents of compliance. You could
hear it in their ears and on their lips. The ears of a
spirited and motivated horse point upward. A horse
comfortable with its leader licks its lips. Grant
contends that the most spirited horses—the ones who
traditional trainers wrote off—have the most potential
if you do the hard work of earning their trust. The
leadership translation: stop beating your rebels and
wildcards into submission, assume they are good, and
watch them contribute in extraordinary ways.

Decades later, the world's most prominent
organizations travel to Jackson Hole to learn not only
what Grant teaches about horses, but what Grant's
interaction with horses teaches about leadership. If
there's one thing Grant wants leaders to take with
them when they leave Diamond Cross Ranch, it's this:

Honor the slightest try and the smallest
change. Make a big deal of it.

---

[68] *Bounce Moments* are points in life where how you see the
world, how you view yourself, or what you believe changes in a
fundamental way.

With every movement of a hoof or wag of its tail, the horse tells Grant something new. He'll take a wild, undisciplined colt, and just listen for awhile. Then Grant will make the horse work—using some magic to make it run around a circular pen for instance. "I try to make the wrong thing hard and the right thing easy. There's no abuse or harm. It's the horse's choice. When he makes the right choice, I release some pressure."

We've seen Grant in action several times. We're not sure exactly what he means by pressure, and our amateur eyes don't come close to picking up on "the right choice," but Grant Golliher sees it all. When a wild horse—one whose behavior Grant is trying to change—makes even the slightest try, a horse whisperer **honors** it. Honor enough attempts, big and small, and the horse learns to trust. He comes to believe he's safe under the leadership of Grant. As soon as an hour later, a completely wild horse will be snuggled up with Golliher, listening to his every instruction. "I never, ever discipline a horse when it's trying to do the right thing—even if it's done the wrong thing."

If you're still with us at this point, you've almost certainly decided to assume positive intent. Like Grant believes in his horses, you believe in your people. You've told them you want them to speak fearlessly, you've jumped in to prove the water is safe, and maybe you even roped off a boundary. Now, you must dignify the slightest admission and make a big deal of the smallest suggestion. Your people's fearless words are flowing freely in a budding culture of candor. Encourage them and celebrate them. Never discipline someone for trying to say the right thing, even if they've said something wrong.

During the summer of 2002, I interned for the Seattle Supersonics in the basketball operations office.[69] There were only four or five of us there on a daily basis: the general manager, the head coach, a receptionist, and my boss, Rich Cho (the assistant GM). I remember Rich as incredibly welcoming. The team president, Wally Walker, had brought me in because "the price was right." (I worked for free that summer, and might not have given them their money's worth.) Rich didn't always know what to do with me. Sometimes I felt bad for him. I spent several days scraping names (of guys who had retired or left the league) off small placards. Then I glued on new letters (incoming rookies) for the upcoming NBA draft. It wasn't lost on me the Sonics were paying benchwarmers millions, and I was contracting carpal-tunnel syndrome recycling one-dollar pieces of plastic. In 2002, the Sonics were six years removed from an NBA championship appearance and five years shy of drafting future hall-of-famer Kevin Durant. Not only did I work for free as a thirty-year-old MBA candidate; I worked for free for a bad team.

To try and make my mark, I went into Cho's office and suggested a potential trade. Think about how ridiculous this is for a second. I was an *intern*. The most important thing I'd done that summer was consolidate the team's salary cap spreadsheets from

---

[69] Seattle once had an NBA franchise.

thirty different files into a single Excel file with thirty sheets. They seriously stood around the computer screen and looked on as if I'd painted the ceiling of the Sistine Chapel. The GM thought I was a genius. I didn't tell him I was undoubtedly the least-competent spreadsheet manipulator at my entire business school. I just reveled in the perceived expertise.

So on the heels of my Excel success, I approached Cho with a thought.[70] The Sonics' franchise player for the last decade had been Gary Payton, but Payton was in his early thirties, and the Sonics were going nowhere. I found some guys on the Cleveland Cavaliers whose contracts would be expiring soon and recommended to Rich that "we" send Payton to Cleveland for an injured Lamond Murray, Michael Doleac, and Brian Skinner or Ricky Davis.[71] Cho looked up from his desk, grimaced and said, "Who?" Then—in a kind way—he started laughing.

My Payton-to-Cleveland idea might have been the worst trade proposal anyone ever floated to a real assistant GM in the history of the National Basketball Association. I can hardly believe I said it out loud. And that's exactly the point. Rich Cho laughed, but he chuckled in such a way I had to smile along. He later came out of his office, tapped me on the arm, and told me he liked the attempt. "Keep thinking about it."

Later that season, the Sonics sent Payton to Milwaukee for a young Ray Allen. It was Cho's idea, and a genius move. He knew his stuff. I only worked

---

[70] Possibly trying to capitalize on the halo effect.

[71] Expiring contracts meant the Sonics could drop them after one year and free up money to sign future free agents.

for Rich Cho for a few months, but I felt I could speak fearlessly to him. He inspired me to continue my quest for valuable ideas. Why wouldn't I?

The Greek word for Cho's graceful response is makrothumia. Makros means "long" and thymus indicates "indignation" or "anger." The literal English translation of makrothumia then is lengthened anger. A more interpretive understanding of the word suggests patient tolerance of incompetence.

As leaders, we build trust when we have a right to show anger or point out the inanity of a statement or idea, but we choose not to. Based on just how bad my trade proposal was, Rich Cho should have mocked me. *"Don't come in here and waste my time with your goofy ideas. You're an intern."* He didn't. Instead, he chose to dignify an idiotic trade recommendation from a guy who should have been across the office scrubbing plastic nameplates.[72] Rich's honoring my nonsensical but honest try—his impressive display of makrothumia—cultivated psychological safety in its purest form.

Trading away the team's best player for almost nothing in return would not have been wise. Cho was right to say, "Who?" and then let me down gently. But we have abundant opportunities to say "Yes" to our people and we pass them by without thinking. Yet every time you say "Yes" or "No" to the people you lead, you make two decisions: a short-term

---

[72] Rich Cho went on to become the first Asian-American GM in the history of American professional sports.

makrothumia:
patient tolerance of incompetence

decision about the idea and a long-term decision about organizational culture. Saying "Yes" waters the roots of fearlessness. Saying "No" (especially without explanation or words of development) gradually erodes the spark of excitement inside eager members of your team.

If it's not life or death, say "Yes."

Life or death in your organization might be compliance, proper accounting procedure, safety, or numerous other non-negotiables. Consider wisely when your teams speak up on the few most critical topics. But more often, we are dealing with other things (important issues, but not life or death). We could take on some risk for the sake of the bigger cultural implications, development of those we lead, and all the ensuing benefits of Say Anything leadership. But we still say no—almost reflexively. Laura Lothrop's boss did it when she said "No" to plant-potting instruction. 3M famously rejected the sticky note concept for *thirteen years*. As parents, we say "No" to our kids all the time, often because it's just easier than saying "Yes." In 2012, we surveyed hundreds of leaders we had worked with over the years. We asked them simply:

"At the times I hold back from speaking candidly to my leader, it's because..."

We expected the overwhelming winner to be "I am afraid of the consequences." That answer finished in third place. By a resounding margin, our respondents first choice was, I hold back because:

"I do not believe it will do any good."[73]

That's a sad commentary on the state of leadership today. Our people are shutting up because they believe speaking up fearlessly is a waste of their time. Don't let it be.

Howard Behar began working at Starbucks in 1989 and took over as company president when the coffee-roaster was still an unknown independent. He spent many of his early days spot-checking operations across the company's expanding footprint. In June of 1994, he traveled to L.A. to check on performance in the southern California region and made a surprise stop in Santa Monica. On that day, every aspect of the store he visited impressed him, with one exception: he was curious why the store had a blender behind the counter. Earlier that spring, an assistant manager named Greg Rogers asked his boss if he could buy the blender and bring it in. Greg wanted to try mixing a cold coffee drink. He'd previously worked at a quirky place called Humphrey Yogart (seriously), and their cold-drink options had people lining the streets in July and August. At Starbucks in Santa Monica, traffic dwindled during these same months. Roger's boss

---

[73]The number two answer in our survey was "I am not sure I am right." People truly are afraid of judgment and disapproval. When we dignify the smallest attempt, we prove it's safe.

was the first person to say "Yes." Greg bought the blender.

So Howard Behar came in and asked about the blender. Greg Rogers poured him a sample of one of the cold drinks, and Behar's face lit up. He loved it. At the next team meeting, Howard Behar floated the idea to Howard Schultz, the CEO of Starbucks and Behar's boss. Schultz said "No." He had two "important" reasons:

1. He didn't like blenders in the stores; they detracted from the coffee ambience.

2. Product development wasn't Behar's job. Starbucks was already working on some cold-drink options in conjunction with Coca-Cola.

Howard Behar initially listened to Schultz, but then dismissed him in favor of listening to his employee. Behar was the second person to say "Yes." He called down to the store manager in Santa Monica and told her to carry on with the drink in a clandestine manner. "Two things," he told her. "First, call me every single night and tell me the results. And second, don't tell anyone else about this."

A few months later, the Frappuccino accounted for forty percent of sales in the Santa Monica store. Behar ordered a test of the concept in a few other markets and ultimately went back to Schultz. "I blew you off. Want to see these numbers?" Four billion dollars per year later, Schultz has Behar to thank. And really, Starbucks should credit Greg Rogers' Say-Anythingminded store manager. She's the one who said "Yes" when Greg asked to buy a blender. She didn't say "Huh?" She didn't say "Just do your job." She didn't delay him and then forget to get back to him.

She said "Yes."

Starbucks dignified Rogers' idea with a five thousand dollar bonus check, a Rolex, and almost legendary status in the late nineties. They made a big deal of it. In the colossal world of Starbucks, Rogers' idea had been a small hunch. But leaders who want to inspire ideas, cultivate candor, and forge fearless cultures must make a big deal of the smallest ideas and the tiniest tries. If you don't, people will give up before they ever get going.[74]

The Frappuccino success is a fun story. We had the privilege of hearing Howard Behar tell it in person when he visited one of our programs a few years back. He buried the punchline in subtlety and followed five minutes of suspense with authentic surprise. His reveal of Frappuccino and four billion dollars per year in revenue created a buzz around the room. But honoring the slightest try must be a leadership habit even when the ideas aren't billion-

---

[74]Money in the blender ©Martin Haas.

dollar ones—even when they're not that good. Even when they are cast-a-chill-over-the-room awkward.

Over two harrowing weeks in October of 1962, the Cold War turned a frightening degree of hot; the world came as close to nuclear war as it had ever been (and hopefully ever will be). In early fall, U.S. suspicions heightened over perceived Russian nuclear activity in the vicinity of Cuba. But Nikita Khrushchev, the Soviet Prime Minister, assured President Kennedy the U.S.S.R would not even consider assembling and arming nuclear weapons on the island. John F. Kennedy's advisors recommended healthy skepticism, yet Kennedy exited September with an admirable but naive trust in his Soviet counterpart. Over the first few weeks of October, definitive photographic proof emerged: Khrushchev and Fidel Castro were conspiring to transport, assemble, and arm nuclear missiles just a few hundred miles off the coast of Florida.[75]

It's almost beyond a matter of opinion: the next two weeks were some of the finest the White House has ever seen. Kennedy led brilliantly through the Cuban Missile Crisis, averting armed conflict and guiding the world to a safety from nuclear disaster that has endured for more than half a century. *It was an exercise in Say Anything leadership.* Having learned from the debilitating unanimity which eventuated the Bay of Pigs debacle, the President demanded a menu of options and an array of dissenting voices. The team in the White House

---

[75] History suggests Castro acquiesced more than conspired.

considered air strikes, air strikes preceded by warning leaflets, an invasion, and several other options. They debated moral questions, strategic issues, and worst-case scenarios. Robert F. Kennedy—the President's younger brother and U.S. Attorney General at the time—described the gravity of the situation: "Each one of us was being asked to make a recommendation which would affect the future of all mankind, a recommendation which, if wrong and if accepted, could mean the destruction of the human race."[76] In other words, cortisol levels were peaking.

As part of the deliberation process, the President stated explicitly he wanted unfettered opinions. He dismissed rank and status and told the group to debate as equals. To make it safe—and to avoid weighing down the group with the anchor of his Presidential opinion—he left the discussions for hours at a time. Ultimately, based on the recommendation of a majority of his team, President Kennedy ordered a naval blockade of Cuba and then massaged his way through frequent communications with Premier Khrushchev and Andrei Gromyko (the less-than-forthright Soviet Foreign Minister). There were more critical choices over the following days, and multiple turning points, but the effective leadership endured. Kennedy navigated the dangerous waters adeptly, doing everything possible to provide the Soviets an "out" and avoid war.

There were many voices from multiple angles. The President filtered the noise and deciphered a solution.

---

[76] From his first-person account in the book *Thirteen Days*.

But this book is not about high-pressure decision-making; it's about the culture you establish which facilitates ideas and solutions. When you truly ask those you lead to Say Anything, you must mean it and dignify even the tries history has proven ill-advised...

Adlai Stevenson, at the time U.S. Ambassador to the United Nations, came down from New York to participate in the missile crisis discussions. He strongly opposed an air strike, and even a blockade, and suggested "we make it clear to the Soviet Union that if it withdrew its missiles from Cuba, we would be willing to withdraw our missiles from Turkey and Italy and give up our naval base in Guantanamo Bay." Those in the room skewered Stevenson for the proposed course of action. It was the 1962 version of negotiating with terrorists. How could he possibly entertain such an idea?

He voiced the option because President Kennedy had cultivated candor—in its most absolute form. Stevenson's idea had immense value—it enabled the President to demonstrate he truly wanted to hear every thought and every notion. John F. Kennedy dismissed the thought of a missile withdrawal and the surrender of Guantanamo Bay, but he dignified Stevenson's try. He shared with the team his own reservations about the value of Jupiter missiles in Turkey and Italy, and explained he had previously asked the State Department to negotiate for their removal. But *now* was not the time—not under duress.

In retrospect, it was a ridiculous idea. What was Stevenson thinking? If we'd given up Guantanamo we'd never have heard Jack Nicholson bark, "You can't handle the truth!" in *A Few Good Men*. Truth, brilliance, or apparent nonsense—dignify every try. That's the brand of leadership which gets people talking and rescues the world from the destruction of nuclear war.

What Rich Cho did with my moronic NBA trade proposal, and President Kennedy did with Adlai Stevenson's suggestion to offer concessions, we must do with every idea: listen to it, consider it, and then—even if it makes us laugh inside—connect with the person who made it, and celebrate the effort. Praise him or her in front of the team, in fact, for being brave enough to speak at all. As Robert F. Kennedy explained later, "Although I disagreed strongly with Stevenson's recommendations, I thought he was courageous to make them."

Someone's idea might go nowhere or it might be the next Frappuccino. Just remember every time you say "Yes," or "No"…every time you nod or shake your head…every time you smile or scowl at the Adlai Stevensons on your team, you forge or weaken your culture of open communication. Even if an idea isn't the greatest, everyone else is watching. When you dignify the slightest try and make a big deal of every fearless word, you empower everyone in your midst—and inside some of them are brilliant ideas.

Bruce Brown has a cult following of fifty-year-old men and women who used to be in his P.E. classes at Hyak Junior High. That loyalty has spawned one-hundred and thirty thousand Facebook followers.[77] Bruce shares wisdom on team-building, leadership, and shared commitment to core covenants. Retired from teaching and coaching, he now consults for the likes of the Philadelphia Eagles, NCAA champion softball and baseball programs, and businesses around the country. "If a mistake is made with carelessness, then take corrective action," Coach Brown suggests, "but if someone makes a mistake with full effort and attention, find a way to dignify the mistake. The bigger the mistake, the more important it is to dignify it."

When the people you lead become fearless in their communication, they are going to make mistakes. They are going to say things the wrong way and ideas that make them look foolish will fly from their mouths. "If someone takes you out of the game when you make a mistake," observes Bruce, "you're going to play not to make a mistake."[78]

Let them play.

Remember Boz? He is the shaven-headed executive at Facebook who told us the only thing you can't say inside their Menlo Park headquarters is "That's just the way we do it." In 2008, as the company's growth accelerated, Andrew Bosworth launched Facebook

---

[77] The Proactive Coaching Facebook page is full of wisdom for coaches, athletes, parents, and leaders. 130k followers was the approximate count when we published.

[78] Bruce also implores us to "never embarrass a willing learner."

Bootcamp—a six-week training program for every one of the company's engineering hires. The *San Jose Mercury News* called it "one part employee orientation, one part software training program and one part fraternity/sorority rush."

Bootcamp differs from its military namesake in one significant way: instructors give the brand new Facebook engineers real software issues they are to debug "in between lectures and other Bootcamp activities." No one at army basic training is darting out of the barracks to participate in a live-fire ambush, but at Facebook the immersion is real. Literally, within two or three days of arriving at the company, certain employees will have written software code which goes live to over a billion worldwide users. The practice reinforces some of the company's cultural proclamations:

Move fast and break things.

Done is better than perfect.

What would you do if you weren't afraid?

In 2010, Facebook threw a complicated software issue at a new Bootcamper. With energy and audacity he attacked the problem and then, before seeking permission, went live with his solution. He crashed the entire site—brought Facebook to its knees for hours and paralyzed hundreds of millions of users (or possibly set them free). "That was a really scary experience for him," empathized Jocelyn Goldfein, a director of engineering at the time. "But no one said, 'You idiot; you don't belong here.' They said, 'Hey, you tried, and here's what we're going to do to try to fix it, and this is what you've learned.' That experience of having people rally around you is really tremendous, and what it teaches you to do is rally around other people."[79]

What would your people say if they weren't afraid?

---

[79] See Mike Swift's April 18, 2012 article in the *San Jose Mercury News*: "A Look Inside Facebook's 'Bootcamp' for New Employees."

12. BE GENUINELY CURIOUS

Listen to everyone in your company and figure out ways to get them talking...
You must listen to what your associates are trying to tell you.
-Sam Walton

Just a few miles south of Facebook headquarters, down California's Highway 101, sits the more humble home of Yahoo! While Facebook spent its first decade vowing to move fast and break things, Yahoo! called upon Marisa Mayer to move fast and fix things. At only thirty-six, she had become the youngest person ever included on *Forbes'* list of most powerful women. Then at thirty-seven, being tabbed CEO of Yahoo! brightened her rising star. Upon graduating from Stanford in 1999, Mayer hitched her trailer to the right wagon. A bachelor's and master's specializing in artificial intelligence garnered her fourteen job offers, including teaching at Carnegie Mellon. She instead chose to become the twentieth employee of a startup called Google. Good choice—for both parties.

Marisa is part Wisconsin, part spunky teenager, and part tech geek. In casual conversation, she throws out a "like" every ten words or so. She's also Chief Executive Officer, super-rich, and on the covers of magazines her employees browse in airport bookstores. She understands the muzzle her own power creates, the need to prove it's safe, and the absolute necessity of tapping diverse viewpoints in

195

her efforts to revitalize the company. When we visited Yahoo!, we heard multiple people rave about the end-of-Friday all-employee gatherings. It was not the gatherings themselves (which have become standard Silicon Valley practice) but Marisa's role in them which stoked excitement. Marisa Mayer—one of the top ten most powerful women in the world—attends every Friday gathering and stays until people are done talking to her. She entertains every voice, hours at a time, until she looks around and no one is left.

"I grew up a big fan of Bruce Springsteen," Mayer explained, "and some time ago I read an article—I think in *Rolling Stone*—where a journalist asked him about his success. Springsteen said he wasn't necessarily better than a lot of other acts in New Jersey (where he started out as a musician), but when he was done with his sets, he'd always hang around and talk to the people at the bar. It built him a loyal following." So Marisa Mayer followed in the footsteps of "The Boss," and decided she'd hang around Friday evenings until people were tired of her. "Not only do I get to talk to people and get to know them," she pointed out, "but I've come across some really important information during those conversations." She's become genuinely curious about what every single person has to say...and for good reason.

At the outset of her tenure at Yahoo!—maybe her third or fourth Friday doing her Bruce Springsteen impression—a woman approached Marisa and complained, "You know, we are getting rid of some really good people."

"I know," Mayer responded. "Unfortunately this transformation comes with re-structuring and cost cuts; we have to let people go."

"Yeah, I get that," the woman replied, "but we are forcing out some of our best talent."

Mayer reiterated her understanding of the situation and suggested uncertainty sometimes scares top talent and they jump at other opportunities. But the employee persisted.

"You don't understand what I'm saying. We are literally laying off some of our **best** talent: on purpose."

Huh? Marisa thought to herself after registering the accusation. "Can you give me a couple examples? I'll look into it." Marisa investigated. The employee was spot on. The Yahoo! Mayer inherited had ample room for improvement in deciding which employees to retain and which it should release. "I decided right then we needed to fix our review process and start taking talent evaluation more seriously. We had inadequate systems for rating our people and determining who were our best performers."[80] One of Marisa Mayer's first major initiatives—implementing quarterly talent reviews—eventuated from the persistence of a concerned employee at a Friday night gathering. Mayer certainly understands the value of exploring the depths. Her practice has inspired ideas which will make or break her efforts to revive the

---

[80] We listened to people at Yahoo! praise Marisa for openness. We also heard complaints about the talent reviews Mayer launched (something she knew would be painful but necessary). Say Anything leadership is not soft. It's well-informed.

company. She also honored the input by taking action, and word spread that the boss listens.

As Marisa Mayer listened to her employee that Friday evening, she undoubtedly processed some first impressions and drew some conclusions:

> *She kind of looks smart? Is she just complaining, or does she know what she's talking about? She's talking with confidence. No way we are laying off our best people. That would make no sense.*

Remember back a hundred pages ago when we explored the topic of judgment and disapproval? None of us are all that good at judging others (especially their intentions). Let's play a little game to reinforce the that idea our mind works in mysterious ways: Please take out a small piece of paper (or write in the margins of the book) and answer this question:

Is the tallest redwood more or less than 1,200 feet?

Tick…tock…tick…Got your answer?

Next question:

What is the height of the tallest redwood?

Nobel Prize-winning economist Daniel Kahneman shares this experiment in his book *Thinking, Fast and Slow*. The question's context is immaterial. It could be

Gandhi's age at his death, the depth of the Marianas Trench, or the length of the Nile River.[81] The peculiarity within the question involves the number of reference: 1,200 feet in this particular case. When researchers asked groups of people if the height was more or less than 1,200 feet, their answers to the second question (the height of the tallest redwood) averaged 844 feet.

Researchers asked separate groups this question:

Is the tallest redwood
more or less than 180 feet?

This group's answers to the follow-on question averaged just 282 feet.

Social scientists attribute the 562-foot gap in responses to the *anchoring effect*. Given even a pinch of mental ambiguity, we subconsciously anchor our thoughts to the number at hand: 1,200 or 180 in the case of the redwood question. "Anchoring effects are everywhere," warns Kahneman. "The psychological mechanisms that produce anchoring make us far more suggestible than most of us would want to be."

In another experiment cited by Kahneman, judges even based their sentencing of a hypothetical shoplifter on literal chance. Experienced magistrates read a description of the thief and then rolled a pair of rigged dice. The dice could land only on three or nine. After each respective roll settled, a judge delivered a ruling. Those who rolled three sentenced the woman

---

[81] 78 years old; 6.831 miles below sea-level; 4,258 miles long.

to an average of five months. Those who rolled nine sentenced her to an average of eight months.

Go back one more time to the murder mystery scenario from Chapter Four. We learned powerful leaders talk too much.

©3dalia

They suffocate the voices of group members and hamper team performance. People don't even fold shirts as efficiently when dominating leaders get in the way.[82] Your power is dynamite; it's a destructive force with a short fuse. When you begin discussions by announcing your own ideas, everyone else shuts up. You have subtly communicated a lack of curiosity about what anyone else might offer up. The team anchors on your suggestion and moves only slightly left or right. Leaders do this all the time, albeit unwittingly. Tomorrow, try it out on purpose—just for fun. Sit down with your team and recommend an off-the-wall or nonsensical idea. Sell it with enthusiasm, and then ask for input. It might go…

> *I'm thinking we should eliminate cheeseburgers from the menu and go with a healthier option like steamed shellfish. What do all of you think?*

Our prediction: a few direct reports will fix their eyes on their laptop screen, a couple more will nod their heads and murmur, and one brave soul—who is silently stewing *this is going to destroy us. It's insane. —*

---

[82] See Adam Grant's entertaining and informative *Give and Take.*

might ask a question: "How do you think that will impact our revenue, boss?"

When leaders go first with our ideas, we anchor the conversation and others instantly become hesitant to wander far from what they think we want to hear. In order to be genuinely curious, you must cast aside your weight and let those you lead launch the conversation. Otherwise, everyone else's response to the redwood question (and all the important things your team needs to discuss) will stay within safe distance of your own answers and opinions.

There's a story in Brad Stone's book *The Everything Store* which explains the author's choice of title. Jeff Bezos—CEO and founder of Amazon—wanted the people around him to execute a grand initiative. Couching it in almost moral terms, Bezos demanded Amazon stock one of *everything*—literally every sellable item on planet Earth.

With apologies to Bezos, the internal "debate" at Amazon regarding this idea is illuminating. People dodged the assignment; they hoped Jeff's fascination would drift away silently; they figured maybe he'd forget over time. The suggestions undoubtedly approached the comical:

"How about almost everything?"

"Anyone know where we can get some reindeer antlers for dogs?"

"You think he'll notice if we can't find a chocolate Kazoobie Kazoo?"

From a guy as powerful as Jeff Bezos, a suggestion like this carries the weight of a multi-ton anchor. It took time, and the specter of more pressing issues, to move on from the idea. But it was painful. Bezos originally dubbed the initiative "the most critical project in Amazon's history."[83]

Bezos is an easy target. He's been wildly successful to the point people write about his heaviest anchors in a book. Back when I commanded an army company, we took a couple weeks to remodel our headquarters area. Some of the stuff involved simple directives like re-painting the word "Integirty" on a set of stairs and replacing a picture of the Secretary of the Army from two terms prior. I didn't need to inspire ideas or cultivate candor. We just had to fix those errors. But in an effort to get involved and share the load, I volunteered to paint the front door. I picked out a color and showed it to my team:

"Sure sir, you're the boss."

"It's different, sir."

By the next day, I'd painted on two coats of shipyard gray. It looked pretty cool—much better than the ugly brown tone I'd covered up. A few days

---

[83] You can read about "Project Fargo" on pages 81-82 of *The Everything Store: Jeff Bezos and the Amazon Age*. The well-written account has a number of Say Anything lessons within.

later our first sergeant and I were coming back from a meeting. "Sir, not sure about that color. It looks like a navy ship. We're in the army." A week later my daughter was born. I took some vacation days to be home with my wife and our three kids. When I returned, the front door to company headquarters had been re-painted the same ugly shade of brown. It was their own way of saying anything.

Instead of throwing out your personal pet notions to kick off discussion, leaders who want their people to Say Anything should ask Authentic Questions. Authentic Questions—like Friday evening meet and greets in the courtyard—engender genuine curiosity.

> An Authentic Question is one where you don't have an answer in mind.

You honestly don't know so you're genuinely soliciting ideas and input. You're genuinely curious. A Spearfishing Question, on the contrary, goes after a specific answer, stymying those you are supposed to be engaging. Spearfishing demonstrates faux interest. It's also self-centered.

(The following scenario is hypothetical):

Jeff: Okay everyone, what's the most important thing we need to do during the next two quarters?

Mike: Solidify our IT infrastructure?

Jeff: Nope. (gripping spear tightly) Not at all. We're solid there. What do you think our *customers* might need?

Beth: Oh! Better service? We could look at re-allocating some of our top talent to customer service leadership positions?

Jeff: No. (agitated and cocking his arm) That's not it. What do you think of our *assortment*?

Pradeep: eBay has an expansive offering. Maybe we should plan a strategic response to their third-party merchant system?

Jeff: No. No. No. No. No! We need to go out and get one of every item on the planet! (thrusting spear into his target)

Jeff's original question looks authentic, but it's not. He has an answer in mind, and he's simply trying to get someone to say it for him. It gets worse from there as the others try to figure out what he's searching for. Spearfishing Questions render people timid and afraid to miss the mark. They are the kiss of death for a teacher in the classroom and a prescription for dry, uninspired conversation in discussions with those you lead. Instead, ask Authentic Questions:

"What led us to miss that number?"

"How can we do better?"

"What was your thought process behind the timing of that launch?"

"What should be our operational focus during the next two quarters?"

"What color should we paint the door?"

Authentic Questions are a critical tool in your quest to inspire ideas and cultivate candor. Don't lead off with your own thoughts. Don't Spearfish for the answers you want. Ask authentically (and tell your people to call you on it when it's obvious you're Spearfishing).

I coached a fourth grade basketball team one year. Nine or ten is about the age you start teaching kids to think critically and make their own decisions on the court. During a scrimmage one evening, a young player named Cade passed up an open shot. I'd been constantly encouraging the kids to shoot when they had a "good look at the basket," and Cade in particular tended to hold back.[84] I almost corrected him: "Cade, take that shot!" But something stopped me. Instead, I asked: "Cade, why didn't you take that shot?" It was an Authentic Question.

Cade lowered his head a bit, looked at me from underneath his eyelids, and grumbled, "Coach, I lost my balance and thought I would miss it. So I passed."

---

[84] Can't knock a player too much for wanting to pass the ball.

I was so glad I asked. I'd come a brain twitch away from taking the easy route: telling Cade what to do. I would have confused him, frustrated him, and missed an opportunity to let him speak fearlessly. I got lucky, really, and I learned a valuable lesson: Authentic Questions are also a critical tool in your quest to forge a fearless culture.

As leaders, we shouldn't have to get lucky like I did with Cade. Just as Grant Golliher can hear a horse's thoughts by watching its ears and lips, we must *really listen* to what our people say. Candid communication won't come in unmitigated form until you've built truly trusting relationships with those you lead. It will start with hints, and we must follow up on those signals with authentic inquiry.

Several years back, I heard a talk by executive coach Marshall Goldsmith. Toward the end of the dialogue, Marshall challenged the group: "How often do you ask your people what you could do better as a leader?[85] Do you ever ask your kids what you could do better as a parent?"

That last part really stuck. I'd never done that before—asked my children how I could be a better father. Goldsmith challenged us to try it, so I texted my oldest son, John. He replied with two words: "You're fine." I figured I wouldn't get much out of John and Jason—both teenage boys. Surprisingly, my chatty daughter didn't offer up much either. But

---

[85] Best-selling authors Barry Posner and Jim Kouzes have access to hundreds of thousands of 360-degree leadership inventories. Historically, "{My leader} asks for feedback on how his or her performance affects other people's performance" is the lowest-scoring item on their survey.

riding in the car with our youngest, Timmy, one day (he was nine at the time), I glanced to the back seat and queried, "Hey Tim-man, what do you think I could do to be a better dad?"

"I don't know," he shrugged. That was that. Then maybe thirty seconds later he spoke up freely. "You know what you could do to be a better dad? You could not kick chairs at basketball games."

Timmy's chair-kicking reference referred to a moment where my wayward foot collapsed a folding chair and rattled a relatively quiet gym. It was almost a humorous incident and happened just once—over a year prior. But if my nine-year-old had anted up some thoughts, I was ready to really listen. I knew there must be more. "Why that, Tim? What didn't you like about that?"

"Well, you know, Dad," he bravely offered in his tiny voice, "you could really be better if you never argued with referees. I feel embarrassed then."

Timmy startled me. I choked up a bit, to be honest. My behavior had shamed him, and continued to do so. If I'd lacked genuine curiosity and stopped at the kicking-chair theme, I'd have never uncovered what he really wanted to say. Watch the metaphorical ears and lips of those you lead, and lead them to deeper revelations. I followed up by dignifying Timmy's try and continue to talk about it with him to this day.[86]

During my first year teaching at West Point, a couple cadets had an idea to start a speaking seminar. Brian

---

[86] My wife, on the other hand, wasn't super impressed. "I've been telling you to stop with that stuff for twenty years."

Shosa, a senior at the time, came to me and grumbled a bit. "We get to hear colonels and generals it seems like every day; it would be really cool if occasionally we heard leadership lessons from business leaders, sports figures, and people like that."

I loved Shosa's idea. We grabbed a junior named Ben Tolle and several other cadets and started to brainstorm. One of our first tasks was to select a name. I'd become really excited about the seminar idea and wrote down several potential winning ideas on a piece of scratch paper.

Brian, Ben, a few other cadets and I gathered in front of a whiteboard one afternoon. Two of the students were freshmen, and Ben wanted them to have a fair shot at naming our new group.[87] He recommended every person submit two ideas, we write them on the whiteboard, and then work from there. So I gathered up the suggestions, placed about ten potential names on the board, and everyone looked at them for a few minutes. I remember thinking the process was kind of a waste. I'd already come up with the perfect moniker.

"Ok," I interrupted, "let's start off by eliminating any names we just can't live with." It took less than two seconds. "That one sucks! Get rid of it." It was mine. Trying not to appear flustered, I moved on. "Okay, what else?"

"Yeah, and get rid of that one too." Brian Shosa pointed to my remaining entry—the one I'd thought

---

[87] At West Point, freshmen—or plebes—will often hesitate to share ideas in front of upperclassmen, much less officers. Ben's instincts were solid.

would carry the day. I don't remember what my submissions were or how the process continued, I just recall the cadets hated my ideas. I was still in my early thirties, but my names resonated as old-guy stupid I guess. Thankfully Ben Tolle had the foresight to make it a blind process, or my suggestions would have been sitting up there until the end, cadets hoping (but not saying) we'd eventually vote them down. After a year and multiple trips with these guys, they'd joke and make fun of my original proposals. But given the military rank structure and fact I'd just met them, no way they would have told me what they really thought of my goofy ideas during our voting exercise.[88]

We came out of the process with a draft title: *The Black and Gold Society*. I ran it by a few colleagues. Bernie Banks—the Apache helicopter pilot who now heads West Point's leadership department—didn't like it. Bernie has a keen sense for brand and marketing. "It sounds secretive; that's not what you're going for." We gave it some more thought and landed on **Black and Gold Leadership Forum**. A couple cadets still preferred the *Society* label, but I made a decision based on hearing from multiple stakeholders.

We fully understand leadership isn't all about asking questions, deferring, and listening. We'd be better off if leaders did **more** of those things, but ultimately leaders have to decide, direct, and execute. Leaders are also held accountable for the results. But

---

[88] If we did it again, I'd give one of the freshmen the whiteboard marker and take a seat among the group.

when gathering ideas, innovating, and developing people and culture, habits like anchoring and Spearfishing are completely detrimental. Be part of the teams you lead, but don't dominate them. And if you want to add value, create blind processes like the one Ben Tolle developed to name the Leadership Forum.[89]

United States Military Academy Department of Behavioral Sciences and Leadership

By the way, because we know you were curious, the tallest redwood in the world has a name—*Hyperion*—and lives in Redwood National Park, California. He's somewhere around six hundred years old and measured 379.7 feet back in 2006. But trees don't hit puberty until they turn seven hundred, so he's still got some growing to do.

---

[89] Kahneman recommends another method based on the *principle of independent judgments*. He suggests team members arrive at meetings having already written a summary of their positions. "The standard practice of open discussion gives way too much weight to the opinions of those who speak early and assertively."

Being genuinely curious is about **how** and it's also about **who** might surprise you with his or her thoughts, ideas, and feedback…

©Natis76

Ralph and Cheryl Broetje's apple business packs more than forty thousand boxes of ripe fruit per day. They farm over six thousand acres, harvest a dozen apple varieties, and employ in excess of one thousand workers year-round and fifteen hundred more during harvest. With a good crop, the company brings in annual revenues surpassing one hundred million dollars. They started this all in 1968 with no farming experience and no money. But selling apples isn't all the Broetjes do. The orchard they built from scratch includes housing for two hundred families, a daycare, an elementary school, a convenience store, a community center, a chapel, and a post office. They've built entire neighborhoods in nearby cities for first-time homebuyers who can't get conventional bank loans, and they've consistently housed hundreds of refugees from all over the world.

The company's nonprofit—the Vista Hermosa Foundation—oversees charities and other efforts in the U.S., Mexico, Kenya, Egypt and the Philippines. Their three decades worth of charitable contributions are just shy of one hundred million dollars. They've led major efforts to establish clean drinking water infrastructures in developing nations and built safe-houses in poverty-stricken areas for young girls whose fate would otherwise likely include a nightly routine involving a pimp and a quota.

Ralph and Cheryl have tended to dying people—literally—alongside Mother Teresa in Calcutta. Cheryl is a self-proclaimed "believer in dreams" and Ralph runs his apple company having never owned a cell phone or a computer. No joke. When they started—the same year the U.S. put a man on the moon—the Broetjes aspired to simply pay their bills. Within a few years they were doing that. A couple more years and they were out of debt and had a savings account. A year later they built a nice big house. And the next year, an even bigger one—this time with an indoor swimming pool. Eventually they built a third house on a bluff overlooking a beautiful river.

In the early 1980s, farming demographics started to shift. Men from Central America began showing up at Broetje Orchards in search of a living wage and a better life. Their native communities south of the border lacked infrastructure. There were no roads to good markets. Many families had been kicked off their land. The water table was horribly inconsistent, and coercive powers and corrupt politicians littered their lives. In the United States, economic conditions had also shifted agricultural practices. Gas prices surged, and migratory farming families that once followed weather patterns across the nation, stopped driving from farm to farm and state to state. By the time they paid for gas and dealt with the costs and stresses of constantly being on the go, the American families were better off heading into cities, settling down, and finding alternative jobs. Almost without warning, farms now desperately needed workers—

such as the immigrants from Central America—to fuel their growing businesses.

In a serendipitously smooth transition, a Latino version of migrant families flooded into the orchards in place of the American one. Business continued to boom for the Broetjes and the new workers drove the success. Soon after this demographic shift, the company started packing its own fruit, adding a plant that could handle high volumes of apples each day. This vertical integration created one hundred new jobs, but the farm already scraped and clawed to fill its picking positions. Sitting on the sidelines was an untapped human resource: women. The Broetjes were soon putting both halves of married couples to work. And as the women became employees, Ralph and Cheryl Broetje started to gather new information. The women spoke candidly, and the information went way beyond apples. The owners learned of ghastly living conditions, mental health situations, domestic violence, and alcoholism. They heard about families sleeping in garages where rats and other rodents bit young children throughout cold winter nights. They learned of older siblings pulled out of school to babysit younger ones while the parents worked. They discovered the high school dropout rate of their employees' children approached eighty percent.

With loads of painful new knowledge, the Broetjes swiftly enacted solutions. They borrowed. They invested. They borrowed some more. They built the on-site daycare center, followed by the initial neighborhood of houses, then a pre-school and elementary followed. This aggressive project continued until they had completed an entire on-site community, outfitted with single-family homes, green belts, after-school programs, sports leagues, and evening potlucks. They capped it off with the Vista Hermosa Foundation—Spanish for *A Beautiful View*—named by the families in their community.

In 1987, inside an apple packing plant near Prescott, Washington, an unexpected spark lit an inferno of unconventional wisdom and compassion that has burned fiercely for nearly thirty years at Broetje Orchards. This spark forever changed the way Ralph and Cheryl ran their company. What began as an entrepreneurial journey to make a little cash has become perhaps the best servant-leadership story on the planet. "We hired mostly women to work in the packing plant," Cheryl explained. "And they began to talk. They spoke up and shared their stories with us. And we listened." It dignified the slightest try in monumental fashion. Imagine the psychological safety imprinted on people's hearts and minds when a leader's response to hearing about biting rats is to build two hundred homes.

The United States Army learned a similar lesson—about untapped pockets of ideas and input—while fighting the War on Terror in Afghanistan. Gathering intelligence in the years following September 11, 2001, Army Special Forces units were underutilizing a full fifty percent of intelligence resources: the women in the villages and towns. Cultural prohibitions against interaction with men constituted an almost impenetrable barrier. Not only was the valuable information these women possessed going to waste, but the enemy effectively spread disinformation among these mothers, sisters, and wives. If the women decided the Americans weren't to be trusted —and told their husbands as much—it could prove a major barrier in working with the Afghan men as well. So in 2011, General Stanley McChrystal launched Cultural Support Teams (CSTs)—small squads of the U.S. Army's most elite women—serving alongside Special Forces operators. The women deployed into the depths of the war and built trusting friendships with the Afghan females who had completely avoided the military men. "CSTs have proven to be a remarkable effects multiplier everywhere they've been employed," observed an Army spokesman a few years later. "They question women, help identify targets, calm tensions, and protect children."

Somewhere amidst the people you lead hides a wealth of untapped potential. As we learned earlier from Deb Gruenfeld: Whether an argument is persuasive is rarely a reflection of its quality; many arguments aren't even heard until the right person makes them. And who are the "right" people? They are those with status, which ends up being fool's gold, because the people who talk the most, talk first, or dress in the right clothes end up gaining influence in the eyes of leaders and team members.

Introverts and newcomers are the packing plant workers and Afghan women of your world—the valuable minds being overlooked.[90] We overlook introverts because they are quiet, and we overlook newcomers because they don't yet know (or so we think). The efficiency of words from introverts and the lack of credibility among newcomers also reduce these people's status—and we know what happens when those without status speak: absolutely nothing. We tune them out. "Our thoughts are shackled by the familiar," observes Jonah Lehrer in his book *Imagine*.[91] Insights on creativity bias we referenced earlier in the book recommended that people disguise their new ideas as old ideas to overcome these shackles.

©Tom Gowanlock

---

[90] For further understanding of these two groups, explore *Quiet* by Susan Cain and *Rookie Smarts* by Liz Wiseman.

[91] Lehrer's book was pulled from distribution channels when he admitted to fabricating quotes from Bob Dylan. He shouldn't have done that, but it's a really good book.

Karim Lakhani of Harvard Business School zeroed in on the problem. "Everyone dislikes novelty," Makhani explained to *The Atlantic*, "[but] experts tend to be over-critical of proposals in their own domain." Our egos get in the way. New ideas—and ideas from new people—suggest perhaps our tried-and-true wasn't good enough. It's a classic cause of resistance to change. Guess what? For the purposes of this book, you're the expert, and your disdain for fresh ideas is killing the spirit of your newcomers. That's a problem, because as Jonah Lehrer and the loads of research he uncovered attest: newcomers have some of the best ideas. They're just not the "right" people.

This is classic organizational behavior. We write off dismissal of these groups as normal and advise the newcomers and the introverts to ally with a person of influence. We tell them to build a coalition with those of status and then pitch ideas or share thoughts, and then we even call this suggestion to play politics mentorship. Work the organization, we counsel, and say the right things in the right way when the time comes. We admit to having no idea how often people successfully pull off these tactics versus how often ideas and suggestions die a sad death born of frustration turned apathy. But here's a question for you:

> Is the number of unspoken (wasted)
> introvert and outsider ideas
> higher or lower than 53%?

Take a shot. We're going with higher.

Experienced leaders sometimes just fail to hear—their dismissal of new ideas isn't even semi-conscious; it's buried deeper. Our familiarity creates a special sort of tone-deafness. Have you ever been on a drive in the car and one of your favorite songs comes on—a classic.[92] You start to sing the first few words and seemingly seconds later the song is over—you missed it entirely (even if you sang along the whole time). This happens to experienced leaders in the realm of new-idea discussions. If we've been around long enough, we listen to people but don't really hear them. Inspire the newcomers and introverts to dive in and you'll hear a whole new song.

We're nearing the end of this book. If you've made it this far, we hope you're writing in the margins, reflecting, and growing as a leader. As you count down the pages, we will make this last point plainly: to draw out your introverts and your newcomers (and those hiding for other reasons we've already covered) you need to do something simple.[93] **Learn who they are**. Don't let them hide, and don't dismiss them because they're not the high-status members of your team. Go get them.

---

[92] For Doug it's Guns N' Roses' "Sweet Child O' Mine." Matt prefers the sweet melody of Jack Johnson's "I Got You."

[93] As we will see in the final chapter, this group also includes those whose quiet stems from cultural difference.

218

IN CONCLUSION

13. THE PROMISED LAND

Vulnerability is our most accurate measurement of courage.

-Brene Brown

Bruce Brown, the legendary coach and teacher we mentioned earlier in the book, has built up a lifetime of wisdom forging fearless cultures. He's coached hundreds of athletic teams ranging from football, to basketball, to baseball, to volleyball. His former players have gone on to play at Harvard, in the NBA, and to coach in the NFL.[94] Like a lot of gym teachers, he's an unbeatable badminton player. One afternoon, about ten years into his education career, he was on his way to a volleyball practice with "bad day" written all over his face. It wasn't a sad sort of bad day; for some reason Coach Brown was just ticked off and annoyed. Janelle, a setter on the team—and by no means the best player—ran by Bruce and patted him on the shoulder. She could sense his mood in the stiffness of her coach's gait. His return greeting to her fell far short of his normal enthusiasm. So fourteen-year-old Janelle stopped on a dime, pirouetted, and looked her coach in the eye: "What's wrong, coach?"

"I'm having a bad day," huffed Brown.

---

[94] Jim Mora, former coach of the Atlanta Falcons and Seattle Seahawks and the current football coach at UCLA.

"How bad?" Janelle wanted to know.

"Pretty bad."

"Well, you know what? I'm sorry about that. But we need you for the next two hours: **Get over it!**"

And then she turned and kept running toward the gym. Janelle was a ninth-grade youngster who believed so much in what the team was doing, she refused to let her coach slide. Through the organization he's built during the second half of his life—Proactive Coaching—Bruce helps teams and businesses develop what he calls "core covenants"— immutable ways of going about their business. That year, the junior varsity volleyball team had agreed upon **enthusiasm** as one of its own covenants. When lived out, it meant every member of the squad would be engaged from the first minute of practice until the last. If players (or the coach) weren't "feeling it," they were to "flip the switch," and engage with full attention at the sound of the first whistle.

"Nobody's exempt from accountability on great teams," challenges Brown. "On that day, Janelle made sure she held me accountable." You don't become weak when you live out Say Anything leadership. Rather, you have to become incredibly strong. Bruce Brown faced the rightful but piercing admonishment of his fourteen year-old volleyball player and had the humility and courage to listen and adjust course. **That** is what an inspiring, cultivating, fearless Say Anything culture looks like.

221

Culture is an important but often misused word. The modern-day authority is Edgar Schein, formerly of MIT.[95] He explains true organizational culture lies in the shared beliefs of group members—what he describes as "basic underlying assumptions." "If a basic assumption comes to be strongly held in a group, members will find behavior based on any other premise inconceivable." Michael Watkins of Harvard argues for a similar understanding, likening culture to an organizational immune system: "It prevents 'wrong thinking' and the 'wrong people' from entering the organization in the first place."

When you've reached the promised land, your people understand it's valued, expected, and safe to Say Anything—anything at all. Wrong thinking consists of hiding thoughts and the wrong people are those who shut down others' voices. Several years back, we learned of an interesting cultural-diagnostic device: Organizational Conversation Killers. What statements—if made among your team, in your office, or around your company— would turn heads and cast a spell of awkward silence across the group? It's an ironic test given the Say Anything concept, but we're talking about just a handful of phrases in any organization.

As an example, let's start with some levity. There's a scene early on in the Christmas classic *Rudolph the Red-Nosed Reindeer* where an angry elf-boss checks in on his toiling-but-joyful North Pole workers. A

---

[95] Schein's a Professor Emeritus from MIT's Sloan School of Management.

golden-locked Hermey's productivity (and attitude) lags behind the other elves, and the boss is not happy. The angry elf questions Hermey—"What's eatin' ya boy?"—leading to a public proclamation of the unthinkable: "I just don't like to make toys."

Hermey's statement jolts Santa's workshop into a quick frenzy. The boss erupts, and the others whisper loudly, "Shame on you!" At the North Pole, the importance of toy-making is a basic assumption. It's what's measured, controlled, and rewarded. The allocation of immense resources (time and material) goes to the production of Santa's loot. Almost nothing Hermey could have said would have revealed the culture more plainly than his declaration he'd prefer another vocation (dentistry) over toy-making. His behavior and thinking was shameful. Here are some additional Organizational Conversation Killers. Match them to the entity on the right...

Can't the customer wait a couple extra days?	United States Marine Corps
I don't really care that much about tradition.	Disney
I'm sick of people smiling all the time.	Walmart
Who cares what Sam Walton said?	Amazon

When your fearless culture arrives, you will know it by the words that shiver the spines of those you lead. They will have come to find "behavior based on {the below} premises inconceivable:"

> "Be careful what you say. The boss doesn't want to hear stuff like that."

> "Learn the ropes and form some alliances before you start speaking up."

> "Whatever you do, don't admit you don't know."

> "Just do your job."

To foster or change culture, Edgar Schein recommends a series of **embedding mechanisms**. Below are a few relevant to building a fearless—Say Anything—culture.[96] They are leadership actions or behaviors we've shared throughout the book, just not in so many words. We embed culture via:

How leaders allocate rewards and status…
What leaders pay attention to…
Organizational systems and procedures…
Formal statements…
Stories about important events and people…

---

[96] Or any culture for that matter.

But most important of all—to this or any culture-forging effort—is the process of deliberate role-modeling, teaching, and coaching.

Which brings us to our final story...

Grainger, Inc. is a business to business distributor operating out of Lake Forest, Illinois. Its nearly 24,000 team members sell roughly ten billion dollars worth of safety gloves, ladders, cutting tools, motors, janitorial supplies, and all kinds of other products each year. It's a wildly successful enterprise with a decades-long track record of rising stock dividends.

Like many corporations, Grainger enlists an external consultant to conduct annual employee engagement surveys. The particular firm Grainger hires services hundreds of other organizations worldwide. The global best benchmark for overall team member engagement—which measures best-in-class companies—is seventy-two percent. Doe Kittay leads the customer service operation at Grainger. In 2014, her organization checked in at eighty-one percent engagement. She's guided a team to an employee satisfaction rate nine percentage points higher than the best-in-class benchmark.[97]

This unparalleled success started out, to some extent, on the first floor of Building B in Grainger's headquarters complex. "I can't really recall any other meeting I've had in the last three years," chuckled Doe, "but I remember that one." She has flashbulb

---

[97] Given this particular consulting firm's measurement scale.

memory, in fact. She can recall what time it was, what she was wearing, where she was sitting, and the ache she felt after receiving the blow. "It felt like a brick in the head, honestly." One of her peers (who would soon become a direct report) had asked for some time to talk. "I want you to know," Brian divulged, "I don't think you value my opinion. I don't even think you like me."

©Les Cunliffe

A really smart British gent Doug taught alongside several years ago developed an insightful model describing how humans respond to feedback. Mark Norton—a former Royal Marine and current HR executive —contends **our instinctive response to another's critique is almost always "Ouch."** No matter how valid the input and how gentle the manner of delivery, we feel an ouch. Sometimes the pain lasts for a few seconds and sometimes a few decades. After we get over the ouch—or even while it's still stinging— we move on to the **It's not my fault** stage, blaming the messenger.[98] In the end, we hopefully settle down and ask: **What can I learn from this?**

---

[98] A final reminder about the difficulty of delivering "bad" news.

The Norton Model™

Ouch!

It's not my fault.

What can I learn from this?

Doe Kittay undoubtedly felt the ouch. Brian's comment hurt. She drifted in her mind to some behaviors he needed to fix—and she eventually shared those—but when Doe came to grips with what her future team member had said, she labeled it a game-changer.

> Brian altered the trajectory I was on. I thought I was good at this aspect of leadership—getting people engaged. I realized I was homogenous in my approach and wasn't reaching everyone. I had a responsibility to reach him in a different way.

> I'll never forget that as long as I live.

Doe knew almost nothing about our book when we sat down to hear her account. We point this out because as she told stories, we realized her success encompassed everything in the preceding pages. She's recognized the suffocating impact of her own power, the bite of past experience, and the fear of judgment and disapproval, and she works tirelessly to overcome these issues. She assumes positive intent, and when her people make an effort, she dignifies the slightest try. Then she unleashes genuine curiosity by asking Authentic Questions of everyone around her.

Most noticeably, Doe proves it's safe. Almost every day, she transparently divulges her inner monologue. "There are some things you have to hold back, but I share just about everything else." In the middle of a complicated and stressful reorganization—one that took close to two years and threatened people's expertise, egos, and livelihood—Doe communicated constantly. She admitted when she didn't know and volunteered her own fears. "I trust people with a lot of information, and that builds trust in return."

"The type of information that gets shared, and with who, sends a powerful message within organizations," explains Sandra Robinson of the University of British Columbia. Confiding in employees with business details, financial results, and other important information not only earns trust, it serves to build trustworthiness.[99] So how do you build a team that trusts you and can be trusted? You trust them first. Sounds a lot like the key to creating positive intent. It's so simple it's almost silly to cite the research. But few people lead this way—otherwise Kittay's team member engagement score wouldn't be such an outlier.

A leader's journey to forge and maintain a culture of fearless communication never really ends. Doe was just six months into her role as Vice President of Customer Service when Brian suggested she didn't value his input. A couple years later, Dave, the person she calls her "right and left hand," stepped into her office. His feedback was unfiltered. It was everything we've claimed leaders should cultivate. Dave told his boss she needed to step up and make decisions. "You can be too inclusive," he warned, "and you need to reign people in and make the call."

"It was hard to listen to," admitted Doe. "I'd asked everyone to let me know what I could do

---

[99] Robinson and her colleague also showed how showering trust on employees led to higher performance, increased ownership, and better financial results.

better as a leader...but it can still be tough to hear. Despite the sting, I thanked him immediately for having the courage to say it."[100] Doe went to sleep that evening, and woke up the next morning, processing what Dave had said. She made small adjustments to her leadership style, and then asked others how she was doing. "I'd call them in after meetings to see how it went in terms of me stepping up to quick decisions."

You may be thinking right now this all sounds somewhat soft—the boss taking it on the chin and adjusting her style based on the input of her team. But we know Delta Force operators (not soft), championship football coaches, and Fortune 100 CEOs who lead this way. It is soft on the outside and strong as steel on the inside. Comfort born of isolation and naivety feels powerful, but it's the ultimate form of weakness.

Doe's not a rock wall—and that's a great thing in so many ways. She's shared her fallibilities. And here's the thing: her employee engagement scores are nine percentage points higher than the next best organization globally and double and triple the worst ones. She's an incredible leader as evidenced by data and the feelings and admiration of those she leads. Her organization thrived through change and continues to accelerate. Kittay's life might be a bit more difficult when people say what they think, but she's a lot better leader because of it—and her team's undoubtedly prospering. Awareness and reflection are difficult. Kittay proves it's safe to speak up,

---

[100] She dignified the try.

attempts to dignify every try, and her curiosity brings forth fresh new voices.

Doe's mom worked in a high school cafeteria and her dad served as a security guard: "The number one leadership lesson I learned from my parents is the value of hard work." Doe is a biracial baby-boomer from Denver, Colorado. Her mother immigrated from Japan after World War II, and her father is of German-Irish descent. Her ethnicity nudged her into four years of involvement with Grainger's Asian Pacific Islander Business Resource Group. She learned more than she taught—learned about a culture whose part she looked but one she'd never really experienced growing up.

"A lot of the people I encountered in the forum had difficulty expressing their opinions in meetings or to their leaders. They thought they'd work hard and get noticed." When that didn't happen as expected, some grew disenchanted. Susan Cain explores this very notion in her best-selling book *Quiet: The Power of Introverts in a World That Can't Stop Talking*. She describes a cultural introversion of sorts based on respected Asian customs: "Talk is for communicating need-to-know information; quiet and introspection are signs of deep thought and higher truth." Cain shares the perspective of a woman whose husband gave up on the culture of verbosity and decided instead to "commute" between Shanghai and California. "In [American] business, you have to put a lot of nonsense together and present it. My husband always just wants to make the point." **Need-to-know**

231

communication, a quiet spirit, and introspection are signs of deep thought and higher truth—a basic underlying assumption.

Kittay spent time trying to help those Asian Pacific Islanders who couldn't quite muster a commute across the Pacific—teaching them how to sell their ideas and accomplishments to those above them. It was helpful in the moment. The individuals suffering the consequences of cultural difference undoubtedly needed the coaching. Doe echoed what Cain explained in *Quiet*: "They are not 'look at me' people." But must we really **recondition** members of our organizations so they can live out their roles as solid contributors to the team?

The need for five-thousand-mile commutes and Doe's work with the API Business Resource Group are exactly what we hope leaders eradicate with a Say Anything perspective. We can teach nurses to communicate positive intent, help people smooth over the rough edges of their words, and provide cultural instruction to an increasingly diverse workforce. Or, we can place the burden on the leader.

Don't make your people figure out how to say things the right way, at the right times, and in the right tone. We're not even suggesting you **make** them say anything at all (despite the title). Rather, **we are passionately encouraging leaders to forge a culture that is all about those you lead and not about you.** Go get those who aren't yet contributing —for whatever reason—and bring them into the conversation in the way that works for them. Not because **they** must, but because **you** and your organization need them. Don't do it through the force of your will, but through the power of your inspiration, authenticity, and curiosity.

Heroic researchers Tost, Gino, and Larrick followed up their murder mystery experiment with another study.[101] They ran a similar problem-solving scenario but instructed certain leaders:

> Everyone has something unique to contribute in this task. Given every team member's unique perspective, obtaining everyone's views of the situation can be critical in reaching a good decision.

There's a confluence here of the Pygmalion Effect, leader power, and genuine curiosity. When told everyone had valuable things to contribute, leaders talked less, made their group members feel more valued, and achieved better results. Here's the deal. Since leaders seem to need a reminder, we're telling you now: Everyone on your team has valuable things to say. Obtaining everyone's views can be critical to leading effectively.[102]

Kittay doesn't need a reminder. She values every voice and seeks each one out. "There are a lot of people who think they don't have anything to offer. If you want to build inclusion, you have to seek them out." Inclusion brings forth creative ideas, newcomer perspectives, and the wisdom of introverts.

---

[101] The follow-up experiment involved reviewing three candidates for an executive position, and making a recommendation to the CEO. One candidate clearly had the best applicant profile.

[102] If that's not the case, find them somewhere else to thrive.

"I ask questions of people who aren't sharing things, but I know they have things to contribute. I can see it in their facial expressions; they might be holding back." Sounds a lot like Grant Golliher tuning in to the ears and lips of his horses. "I don't do it in a negative way," Doe explains with a concerned voice. "I say stuff like, 'I noticed you reacted to that, what's on your mind?'"

We learned of Doe Kittay through Jennifer Porter, a world-class executive coach who founded the Boda Group.[103] Jennifer conducted a unique version of a 360-degree review with Doe's team. The methodology came at Kittay's request. She asked for her team to meet with Jennifer collectively and provide feedback in a team setting (minus Doe). After Jennifer gathered all the input, they would break for an hour and then turn right around and have a candid discussion with Doe in the room. It's a growing trend and a great idea.[104] But Doe's direct reports were confused. They didn't understand the need..."We can tell her anything, anytime—anyway. We don't need to do this."

That's the promised land.

About halfway through the first decade of this millennium, two experienced leaders stood on a Portland, Oregon stage addressing a crowd of eight

---

[103] Jennifer is also the author of our Foreword and made heroic contributions to this book.

[104] A super way to prove it's safe.

hundred first responders from up and down the west coast. One of the gentleman speaking that day was Bruce Brown of Proactive Coaching; the other was Captain (Ret.) Scott Waddle—one-time commander of the USS Greeneville. Captain Waddle shared hard-learned but valuable lessons from his submarine's tragic and fatal collision with the Japanese fishing boat Ehime Maru. Meanwhile, Coach Brown—having never heard of Scott Waddle or the Greeneville prior to that day—passionately championed ideas from his long-standing talk, The Impact of Trust:

> If we wait until there's a crisis to look each other in the eye and tell the truth, we are all in trouble.

Don't wait another day. Forge a culture of fearless communication, and do it now. The work is hard and humbling, but the benefits are immeasurable.[105]

---

[105] If you'd like to Say Anything about our book, please email doug or matt @bluerudderleadership. com. Even if it causes an Ouch, we'll assume positive intent.

EXTRA:

key points,
reflection questions,
and reference notes
for each chapter

CHAPTER 1: THE RIGHT DECISION

So what?

People will hesitate to communicate candidly with you. They'll hold in their ideas, critiques of your ideas, requests for help, confessions of confusion, observations of mistakes, and will even (or especially) withhold calling out lapses of integrity.

When people hesitate to share their thoughts, the behavior becomes contagious and can permeate entire organizations.

Loads of empirical research shows candid communication enhances innovation, ownership, engagement, and overall performance.

As best-selling author and scholar Jim Collins asserts, "Leadership is about creating a climate where the truth is heard."

Personal reflection...

When have you faced a critical moment—in your personal or professional life—and you spoke candidly to someone in power? What was the result?

Leadership reflection...

How would you have responded to Steven Hauschka if you were the coach? Even if you're not a football fan, consider your response (both emotional and verbal) to a fairly junior employee questioning your decision at a critical juncture.

When was the last time someone you led spoke up candidly about your ideas, actions, or guidance? What was your response? (Hint: if you can't think of an example, it might be a sign....)

Rate the level of idea-generation, candor, and fearlessness on a team you lead. What percentage of this rating would you attribute to your team's character and personality, and what percentage would you attribute to your leadership?

Notes—Chapter 1

1. **Mutltipliers don't focus on what they know...**Liz Wiseman and Greg McKeown, *Multipliers* (New York, NY: Harper Business, 2010), p. 138. The original quote is slightly different. Without altering the context, we removed two sentences for brevity.

2. **I didn't think it was the right decision...** Driadonna Roland, "Steven Hauschka makes the right call not attempting 53-yard FG," January 21, 2014. See: http://www.nfl.com/news/story/0ap2000000316345/article/steven-hauschka-makes-right-call-not-attempting-53yard-fg

3. **Direct reports of Carroll...**insight gathered from credible sources on the sideline.

4. **I love the honesty...** Bob Condotta, "Seahawks kicker Steven Hauschka says going for it right call," January 23, 2014. See: http://seattletimes.com/html/seahawks/2022741216_seahawksnotebook24xml.html

5. **Which head coach...** Terry Blount, "Pete Carroll voted most popular," January 28, 2014. See: http://espn.go.com/nfl/playoffs/2013/story/_/id/10363366/pete-carroll-seattle-seahawks-voted-coach-most-players-play-espn-survey; Chart used with permission of ESPN.

6. **Leadership is about creating a climate...** Jim Collins, *Good to Great* (New York, NY: HarperBusiness, 2001), p. 74. Chapter 4 of *Good to Great* is a veritable treatise on Say Anything leadership. Within, Collins recommends four steps to create a climate of truth-telling:
   a. **Lead with questions, not answers**
   b. **Engage in dialogue and debate, not coercion**
   c. **Conduct autopsies without blame**
   d. **Build "red flag" mechanisms**

7. **For further reading on incidents mentioned:**
   a. **Launch of Obamacare Website...** Gloria Borger, "How could Obama not have known," November 14, 2013. See: http://www.cnn.com/2013/11/14/opinion/borger-obama-clinton/
   b. **Space Shuttle Disasters...** "Shuttle report blames NASA culture," August 26, 2003. See: http://www.nbcnews.com/id/3077541/ns/

technology and science-space/t/shuttle-report-blames-nasa-culture/#.VGKyjIc-DBI

c. **Jerry Sandusky's crimes at Penn State...** Malcolm Gladwell, "In Plain View," *The New Yorker,* September 24, 2012.

d. **Watergate scandal...** Jerry Harvey, "The Abilene Paradox: The Management of Mutual Agreement," in *Classics of Organizational Behavior, Third Edition,* Walter Natemeyer and J. Timothy McMahon, eds. (Prospect Heights, IL: Waveband Press, 2001), pp. 224-240.

e. **Snapple acquisition...** Chip Heath and Dan Heath, *Decisive* (New York, NY: Crown Business, 2013), pp. 35-36.

CHAPTER 2: ANOTHER OPTION

So what?

SAY ANYTHING is a leadership book about YOU and puts the responsibility for creating a culture of fearless communication directly on your shoulders.

Candid communication oftentimes uncovers solutions nobody could see before. There's power in boldness, and sometimes bluntness.

When people in your organization don't speak up, it's not their problem—it's yours.

Three dynamics impede candid communication:

1. the leader's power
2. the sting of past experiences
3. fear of judgment and disapproval

The three things leaders must do to overcome these obstacles are:

1. prove it's safe to speak fearlessly
2. dignify the slightest efforts when people say what they are thinking
3. be genuinely curious and empower the candid communication of everyone around

Personal reflection...

What would have happened (in your organization) if Jeff Gaines had said to his boss: "I don't know what to do. I need your help." Do you feel comfortable asking for help or admitting uncertainty? Why or why not?

Leadership reflection...

What would you have told Jeff Gaines if you were his boss, and he came to you for help? (Not about merchandising but about his competing interests.)

When was the last time a member of your team came to you for guidance or to admit he or she didn't know what to do? What happened? (Hint: if you can't think of an example, it might be a sign.)

On a scale of 1-10, how much do you buy into the idea that Jeff should have "another option"— speaking candidly to his boss? Explain your rating: if it's above 5, discuss what you need to change to fully live out the notion of Say Anything leadership. If 5 or below, explain your reservations about the concept.

CHAPTER 3: IN THE TANK

Personal reflection...

Consider a time you felt powerless, judged, or suffocated. Tell the story. What does it feel like—literally in your body—when you are facing really intense pressures? What are the contributing factors causing these pressures?

Leadership reflection...

On a scale of 1-10 (1 being low and 10 being high), rate your shark-like tendencies. Do you make people nervous? Why or why not?

On a scale of 1-10, how would the people you lead answer the same question? Explain the similarity or difference in the ratings.

As a leader, have you recently questioned someone's intentions or judged that person's words critically? Tell the story. How did you resolve your speculation? Did you discuss it with the person you lead? Why or why not?

CHAPTER 4: SUFFOCATING POWER

So What?

Powerful, formal leaders hamper team problem-solving. The mere presence of a leader hinders a group's ability to think creatively and speak openly.

Leaders who feel powerful wreak havoc—stereotyping more and listening less.

Leaders talk too much—dominating discussions, shutting others down, and devaluing input. If your goal is to look good, then by all means talk a lot. If performance is what you're after, encourage others to speak up.

Leaders must work tirelessly to mitigate the unintended effects of their power.

Personal reflection...

What would you like to say to your boss but haven't had the courage to express? What do you believe are the potential consequences if you told your boss exactly what he or she needs to hear? What would be the benefits?

Leadership reflection...

On a scale of 1-10, how powerful are you in your current leadership role? To what extent is your power shutting down those you lead?

Who on your team are you stereotyping? Who have you dismissed and shut down?

When was the last time someone you lead said something strikingly candid to you? (Hint: if you can't think of an example, it might be a sign.) What was your response inside your own head? What was your outward response? If they were different, why? If they were the same, why?

Notes—Chapter 4

1. **Personalities change when the President...** Robert F. Kennedy, *Thirteen Days* (New York, NY: W.W. Norton & Co., 1971), p. 27.

2. *The Case of the Fallen Businessman...* Special thanks to Gary Stasser of Miami University (OH) for sharing his murder mystery scenario. Stasser first used the scenario in 1992 as part of a series of studies on group communication. For further reading on the topic, see: http://www.spring.org.uk/2009/08/why-groups-fail-to-share-information-effectively.php

3. **People tend to share common knowledge...** also from Stasser. Further reading at link immediately above..

4. **Power causes a leader to objectify others...** Deborah H. Gruenfeld, M. Ena Inesi, Joe C. Magee, and Adam D. Galinsky, "Power and Objectification of Social Targets," *Journal of Personality and Social Psychology,* 95, no. 1 (2008): 111-127.

5. **It creates tone deafness...** Francesca Gino, Richard P. Larrick, and Leigh Plunkett Tost, "When Power Makes Others Speechless: The Negative Impact of Leader Power on Team Performance," *Academy of Management Journal* 56, no. 5 (2013): 1465-1486. Gino et al. cite others' research on these points; we take their word for it.

6. **More prone to stereotype...** ibid.

7. **Less likely to listen...** ibid.

8. **Solved the mystery sixty-two percent of the time...** email exchange with Francesca Gino, November 2014.

9. **I constantly have discussions with my team...** this was a brave admission by a highly successful leader in a Fortune 100 company.

10. **Professor Adam Grant calls these power-filled leaders** *takers...* Adam Grant, *Give and Take* (New York, NY: Viking, 2014), p. 147.

11. **Secretly, the researchers had placed some 't-shirt folding experts...'** ibid., p. 148. Francesca Gino also participated in this research with Grant. She's the MVP of our book.

12. **Planes are safer when the least experienced pilot is flying...** Malcolm Gladwell, *Outliers,* (New York, NY: Little, Brown and Company, 2008), p. 197. Gladwell goes on to describe a

study involving "six levels of mitigation": **command, obligation statement, crew suggestion, query, preference, and hint.** When surveyed, captains overwhelmingly said they would "command" to avoid storms seen on the radar. First officers, however, overwhelmingly said they would "hint."

13. **The *USS Greenville*...departed for standard maneuvers...** National Transportation Safety Board Marine Accident Brief; Accident No.: DCA-01-MM-022, May 2001. See: www.ntsb.gov/investigations/fulltext/mab0501.htm

14. **What the hell was that...** ibid.

15. **Scott Waddle graduated...** "10 years later—Japanese Continue to Mourn Their Loss—Ehime Maru Sinking," February 10, 2011. We don't know Scott Waddle, but we do know what it feels like to fail. In 1996, I almost fired a tank round into an infantry company maneuvering through the woods of Ft. Polk, Louisiana. We withhold judgment and share the *Greeneville* story entirely with the hope *Say Anything* leadership will make a real difference in the future. See: navycaptain-therealnavy.blogspot.com/2011/02/japanese-continue-to-mourn-their-loss.html

16. **The moment a leader allows himself...** Jim Collins, *Good to Great* (New York, NY: HarperBusiness, 2001), p. 72.

CHAPTER 5: ONCE BITTEN

So what?

We start out life candid and eager but learn—through painful experiences—to measure our words and speak cautiously (or not speak at all).

Culture teaches us what's safe and acceptable, and what's punished and rewarded. It also teaches us what not to say.

Far too many people are keeping their brilliant ideas to themselves, and it's a leader's responsibility to overcome this.

Personal reflection...

Consider a time you received a smackdown that left you afraid to speak up. How did you move past it, or how does the sting still hold you back from speaking candidly?

Leadership reflection...

When have you shut someone down and later realized you led poorly? How did you reconcile the situation, or have you?

As a leader, what idea have you opposed which later proved to be something you were wrong about? How did you respond, and what did you learn from the situation?

Who on your team seems hesitant to speak up? What might be the reason? How much do you know about his or her past experiences?

Notes—Chapter 5

1. **How schools kill creativity...** Sir Ken Robinson, see: http://www.ted.com/talks/ ken_robinson_says_schools_kill_creativity?language=en

2. **The lieutenant colonel surveyed the readiness...** interview with unnamed army officer, October 2014.

3. **Each year 1 in 20 patients...** David Maxfield, Joseph Grenny, Ron McMillan, Kerry Patterson, and Al Switzler, "Silence Kills: The Seven Crucial Conversations in Healthcare," (Vital Smarts, 2005).

4. **The surgeon was at a dinner party...** David Maxfield, Joseph Grenny, Ramon Lavandero, and Linda Groah, "The Silent Treatment," (VitalSmarts, 2010). These two healthcare studies —in conjunction with other research we read on organizational silence from Frances Milliken, Elizabeth Morrison, and Patricia Hewlin ("An Exploratory Study of Employee Silence")—establish that there is an indisputable communication issue across a spectrum of organizations: people are afraid or unwilling to speak up. While VitalSmarts likely does outstanding work teaching people upward communication in the face of obstacles, the more powerful and efficient solution is effective leaders who welcome input in all the ways **SAY ANYTHING** suggests.

CHAPTER 6: FEAR OF JUDGMENT

So what?

Fear of judgment impedes those we lead from saying what they think.

A leader's judgment and disapproval extinguishes ideas, feedback and requests, and can sometimes completely paralyze people from thinking logically and/or rationally.

Evaluation anxiety induces increased levels of cortisol—the stress hormone.

People are so concerned about their image and the impressions they make that they fear asking for help, admitting errors, or seeking feedback—even when it will benefit the organization. They'd rather *save face* than risk being viewed in a negative way.

Leaders hear their high-status people—both more often and in a more receptive way. Many arguments aren't even heard until the right person makes them.

People who speak first, often, and assertively gain status.

There's no correlation between being the best talker and having the best ideas.

The more powerful people become, the less they consider facts, evidence, and well-rounded input, favoring instead (usually unknowingly) subjective items that have little to no relevance to the decisions they are making.

Personal reflection...

When have you chosen to keep your image "safe" instead of telling your boss how you really felt about something? Was it the right decision or did you regret staying quiet?

Leadership reflection...

Consider the team you lead. Who has high status in your eyes and why? Who has low status and why? How does your opinion of your people impact their contributions to team conversations?

Who on your team talks the most? Who talks the least? How does their level of input correlate with the quality of their ideas? Who on your team would you like to hear more from, and what can you do to help?

As a boss, coach, teacher, leader, or volunteer, consider someone you've led who exceeded your expectations or who proved different than what you had heard. Why did this person perform better than expected? Did the person up his or her game, or were the expectations wrong? Or something else?

Notes—Chapter 6

1. **"Abilene Paradox,"** ibid. We built this narrative entirely from Jerry Harvey's original work as found in *Classics of Organizational Behavior.* The notion of the Abilene Paradox is often misused in popular literature. The key to the idea is a selected course of action must be **no one's preferred option,** yet the group still chooses it. It's entirely a result of individuals failing to speak up candidly.

2. **What on earth would it have taken to decide against the Watergate plan…** ibid.

3. **I don't know why I lied just then…** *Moneyball,* Sony Pictures, 2011.

4. **People fear asking for help…** Amy Edmondson, "Psychological Safety and Learning Behavior in Work Teams," *Administrative Science Quarterly* 44 (1999): 350-383.

5. **Evaluation apprehension is anxiety…** *Oxford Dictionary of Psychology.* See: http://www.oxfordreference.com/view/ 10.1093/acref/9780199534067.001.0001/ acref-9780199534067-e-2909

6. **Goleman illustrates the neurological mechanics at work…** Daniel Goleman, *Social Intelligence* (New York, NY: Bantam, 2007), pp. 272-274.

7. **They were floating gently down the river…** Daniel Kahneman, *Thinking, Fast and Slow* (New York, NY: Farrar, Straus and Giroux, 2011), pp. 79-80.

8. **Friendliness is perceived as inversely related to competence…** Craig Lambert, "The Psyche on Automatic," *Harvard Magazine,* November-December, 2010. This article profiles Harvard professor **Amy Cuddy.** See: http:// harvardmagazine.com/2010/11/the-psyche-on-automatic

9. **Beware the halo effect…** ibid.

10. **If we see a person first in a good light…** "The halo effect," *The Economist,* October 14, 2009. See: http:// www.economist.com/node/14299211

11. People evaluate others' competence in less than… We heard **Deb Gruenfeld** explain this in person when she visited one of our programs. You can hear it here: https:// www.youtube.com/watch?v=KdQHAeAnHmw

12. **You'll be looking for input…** Kahneman, p. 81.

13. **Because the above statement is in bold…** ibid. p. 63.

14. **Higher status on those who speak...** ibid. p. 85.

15. **The culture of many organizations suppresses...** Dan Lovallo and Olivier Sibony, "The case for behavioral strategy," *McKinsey Quarterly*, March 2010, p. 9.

16. **Guys who are dads get a status bump...** Amy Cuddy in Craig Lambert, *Harvard Magazine*.

17. **Peter DeMarzo** is the Mizuho Financial Group Professor of Finance at the Stanford Graduate School of Business.

18. **The selection of stocks is more like rolling the dice...** Kahneman, p. 215.

19. **The success of venture capital...** Cuddy via Lambert.

20. **Whether an argument is persuasive...** Notes taken from leadership seminar with Deb Gruenfeld.

21. **People make inferences of competence based on...** Cuddy via Lambert in *Harvard Magazine*.

22. **Those who talk the most...** Kahneman.

23. **There's zero correlation between being the best talker...** Susain Cain, *Quiet* (New York, NY: Broadway Books, 2013). We couldn't find this exact quote in her book, but she did say it in her TED talk: http://www.ted.com/talks/ susan_cain_the_power_of_introverts/transcript? language=en. Although we explored much of the original research on our own, we sincerely thank Susan Cain's book for leading us to evaluation apprehension, fear of judgment, and Adam Grant's t-shirt folding experiment.

CHAPTER 7: THE POSSIBILITIES

So What?

When leaders create an environment where people speak fearlessly, ideas thrive, sacred cows die, and decisions improve.

Dialogue, debate, skepticism, and scrutiny influence successful decision making six times more than pure analysis.

Trying to find the right way to say something to a boss significantly hinders a person's ability to think creatively.

In general, we hold a bias against creative thinking. Leaders need to listen actively instead of formulating a rebuttal as they selectively listen.

Personal reflection...

When have you tried to word something exactly right to your boss, only to have it come out all wrong? What pressures caused you to be so concerned about the way you said it? Were you able to recover and convey what you were aiming for?

Leadership reflection...

What is one personal "blind spot" you've been made aware of by someone you lead? Have you ever asked members of your team for feedback on how you could lead more effectively? (Not including mandatory 360 evals.) Why or why not?

When did you thoroughly analyze a situation on your own—covered all aspects—and made the "best" decision given all the data, but it turned out to be a terrible one? What did you overlook and how might others have helped you get it right?

How creative are you? (No 1-10 scale this time; instead be *creative* in your answer.) Who's the most innovative person on your team and how well do you relate to him or her? What's the best idea a member of your team has ever come up with?

Notes—Chapter 7

1. **Had not called them together to ask their advice...** Doris Kearns Goodwin, *Team of Rivals* (New York, NY: Simon and Schuster, 2005), p. 464. Further research on the Emancipation Proclamation decision came from Goodwin's interview with NPR on November 15, 2012. See: www.npr.org/2012/11/15/165220138/doris-kearns-goodwin-on-lincoln-and-his-team-of-rivals

2. **Investigated 1048 business decisions...** Ovallo and Sibony, ibid. p. 5. This is a superb paper on strategic decision-making. In conclusion, the authors recommend four steps to ensure leaders ferret out biases and make sound choices: **1. Decide which decisions warrant the effort, 2. Identify the biases most likely to affect critical decisions, 3. Select practices and tools to counter the most relevant biases, and 4. Embed practices in formal processes.**

3. **Good analysis in the hands of good managers...** ibid.

4. **We prefer known solutions...** Jennifer S. Mueller, Shimul Melwani, and Jack A. Goncalo, "The Bias Against Creativity: Why People Desire But Reject Creative Ideas," *Journal of Psychological Science* 23 (2012), no. 1, pp. 13-17.

5. **American culture worships creativity...** Derek Thompson, "Why experts reject creativity," *The Atlantic*, October 10, 2014. See: http://www.theatlantic.com/business/archive/2014/10/why-new-ideas-fail/381275/

6. **Trying to find the right way to say something...**Daniel Pink, *Drive* (New York, NY: Riverbed Books, 2011).

7. **Sometime prior to 1993, Pacific Power and Light...** Elaine Camper, April 2, 1993. See: http://www.insulators.info/articles/ppl.htm

8. **The curse of knowledge...**Chip Heath and Dan Heath, *Made to Stick* (New York, NY: Random House, 2008), p. 19.

9. **Boz has been at Facebook since close to the beginning...** talk at Facebook headquarters, spring of 2013.

10. **I have always just believed in transparency...** Jessica Guynn, *Los Angeles Times*, "Profile: Andrew Bosworth, Facebook social engineer," July 31, 2011. See: http://articles.latimes.com/2011/jul/31/business/la-fi-himi-bosworth-20110731

CHAPTER 8: CENTER OF GRAVITY

Leadership reflection...

What is the Center of Gravity of your company, team, or organization? What is holding it together? What might competitors take aim at?

What is the Center of Gravity of your leadership philosophy? How do you decide what's most important as a leader?

Who advises you on key leadership ideas and what's the best advice he or she has provided?

CHAPTER 9: POSITIVE INTENT

So what?

Leaders can create positive intent by assuming it. We assume intent anyway—positive or negative—so it sounds fairly easy. But it's truly difficult to make the critical shift needed to assume it all the time—from everyone.

The Pygmalion Effect—the empirically proven idea that how we think has a causal effect on how our people perform and behave—has far-reaching implications for Say Anything and leadership in general.

To forge a fearless culture, you must truly believe in those you lead. Change the way you think and it will change everything. Perhaps to your surprise, it will change the intent of the people who follow you. Sounds crazy, but it's proven.

Disentangle impact from intent.

Release people from the burden of saying things the "right way."

Personal reflection...

Who believed in you, and how did it change who you are or how you perform(ed)?

Leadership reflection...

Who have you believed in and how do you think it changed that person? (Brag a bit.)

Of whom do you have low expectations? Who do you hold in a dark light—assuming the person will just mess things up? How much of his or her performance is a result of your beliefs? How could you change course? Or can you?

Do you think you can or will assume positive intent and "never meet a bad member of your team"? Why or why not?

Notes—Chapter 9

1. **If someone doesn't trust you...** from an interview with Bruce Brown at his house on Camano Island, Washington, October 2014.

2. **Earn the right to be heard...** See: http://www.younglife.org/About/Pages/History.aspx

3. **They begin by explaining...** *The Silent Treatment*, p. 7.

4. **Disentangle impact from intent...** Douglas Stone, Bruce Patton, and Sheila Heen, *Difficult Conversations* (New York, NY: Penguin Books, 1999), p. 54.

5. **In 1966 J.R. Burnham injected...** Robert Rosenthal and Lenore Jacobson, *Pygmalion in the Classroom* (Bethel, CT: Crown House Publishing, 1992). The overview of the rat experiment and studies at the Oak Hill School came entirely from this book.

6. **The Pygmalion Effect is the most...** Snook has presented for us multiple times—at Harvard Business School, at West Point, and in Washington State. We took this quote from a November 2014 phone interview. Snook also recommended the General Schwarzkopf example.

7. **In 1982, Eden gained access to an Israeli Defense Forces...** Dov Eden and Abraham B. Shani, "Pygmalion Goes to Bootcamp: Expectancy, Leadership, and Trainee Performance," *Journal of Applied Psychology* 67 (1982), no. 2, pp. 194-199.

8. **They were quite good leaders...** Dov Eden, "Leadership and Expectations: Pygmalion Effects and Other Self-fulfilling Prophecies in Organizations," *Leadership Quarterly* 3 (1992), no. 4, pp. 271-305. The best paper we've read on the Pygmalion Effect and all its implications. What Francesca Gino and her colleagues contributed to our understanding of power and its impact on communication, Dov Eden has done for our further understanding of self-fulfilling prophecies.

9. **We are going to borrow a story...** ibid.

CHAPTER 10: PROVE IT'S SAFE

So what?

Tell your people explicitly to share their thoughts and ideas—verbalize that it's safe, or it *won't be.*

Body language tells others whether or not it's safe to share ideas and communicate candidly.

Vulnerability begets trust. **Jump in first** if you want others to dive in and speak candidly. Sharing your own thoughts shows people you're willing to take the plunge. They will follow your lead.

In your effort to get those you lead to speak up, **rope off a boundary**. This entails the delicate balance between providing enough parameters for people to feel safe, but not so many you smother them.

Personal reflection...

How safe is it for you to speak up at work? What are the most important dynamics contributing to your answer? What's the safest you've ever felt in terms of communicating with a boss? Why was this boss so effective in gaining your trust?

Leadership reflection...

Do you want your people to Say Anything? Why or why not?

If you're all in on the idea of candid communication, how can you prove it's safe? Seriously, right now, tomorrow, whatever, what can you do to inspire ideas and cultivate your people's input? What story can you share? What things can you say to begin forging a culture of fearless communication?

Have you ever apologized to anyone you lead? Tell the story. Have you ever told your team you were wrong or didn't understand? Why or why not (assuming you've ever been wrong or didn't understand something)? How did it feel?

Notes—Chapter 10

1. **Shoes, sir. The men need...** *Glory*, Tri-star Pictures, 1989.
2. **WADOT is attempting to recruit and retain...** Phone interview and follow-up email with Nicole House. November, 2014.
3. **There are few things more liberating...** Conan O'Brien. See: https://www.youtube.com/watch?v=KmDYXaaT9sA
4. **Leaders must facilitate vital...** Amy Edmondson, ibid.

CHAPTER 11: DIGNIFY EVERY TRY

So what?

To forge a fearless culture, dignify the smallest ideas and quietest comments people put forth—make a big deal of these efforts.

When your people make a request, float an idea, or offer a suggestion, if it's not life or death, say "Yes."

Every time you say "Yes" or "No" you make a short-term decision about the idea and a long-term decision about culture.

Most people who don't speak candidly to their boss hold back because they "do not believe it will do any good."

Celebrate willing learners who make mistakes with full attention and effort.

Personal reflection...

When was the last time you said or did something really dumb? How did your leader respond?

Leadership reflection...

The last time someone brought you a suggestion, did you say "Yes," or "No"? Why? If you said "No," what would have needed to be different for you to say "Yes"? Share a different story about a time you welcomed another person's perspective, and made a change because of it.

Consider the most recent time someone on your team took a shot at an idea, made a suggestion, or offered an opinion—and it was **really bad.** How did you respond? How do you think your response impacted the trust dynamic between that person and you?

Do you buy the idea that each "Yes" and "No" has long-term cultural implications? Why or why not?

Notes—Chapter 11

1. **Horses can really dig...** This narrative is based on two days I spent with Grant and Jane Golliher at their Jackson Hole ranch in the spring of 2010. We've subsequently used Grant in our leadership programs.

2. **The Greek word...is makrothumia...** we explored multiple websites to settle on an accurate translation of this word. Most of them were Biblical scholarship-oriented, helping pastors prepare sermons and such. Thanks to **Bruce Brown** for introducing us to this word and its application to proving it's safe.

3. **Greg wanted to try mixing a cold coffee drink...** Lesley Balla, "The birth of the Starbucks Frappuccino, Right Here in Santa Monica," June 17, 2008. See: http://la.eater.com/2008/6/17/6793363/exclusive-the-birth-of-the-starbucks-frappuccino-right-here-in-santa

4. **So Howard Behar came in and asked about the blender...** Behar visited one of our leadership programs in 2012. He shared this story and also tells it in his book: *It's Not About the Coffee*. Howard Schultz shares a version in his own book, from what we understand.

5. **Andrew Bosworth launched Facebook Bootcamp...** Mike Swift, "A look inside Facebook's 'Bootcamp' for new employees," *San Jose Mercury News,* April 18, 2012.

6. **Over two harrowing weeks in October...** Kennedy, *Thirteen Days.* The account of the Cuban Missile Crisis and quotes within were all sourced from this book. It's a short, valuable read—unique because of its primary nature.

CHAPTER 12: BE GENUINELY CURIOUS

So what?

The way in which questions are asked and ideas are stated greatly influences how people respond to them, regardless of the content.

As leaders, when you begin discussions by announcing your own ideas, everyone else shuts up. The people around you *anchor* to what you've stated and only move away from it incrementally. Their original ideas have taken a back seat—and they're not moving up a row, at least in that conversation.

Leaders who want their people to Say Anything should ask Authentic Questions—questions where you don't have an answer in mind when posing them. Spearfishing Questions—on the contrary—stifle conversation.

We overlook introverts because they are quiet, but they often have a wealth of untapped potential. We overlook newcomers because they have not yet gained status, but research shows their outsider perspective provides some of the best ideas.

Personal reflection...

If your CEO (or organizational leader) had meetings every Friday afternoon, what would you tell him or her while drinking a beer (or a Coke or water)? Would you Say Anything? Why or why not? If you're the CEO (or person in charge) are you having these conversations, and what have you learned from them?

Leadership reflection...

What's one of the worst ideas you've ever had as a leader? How did your people respond to it? (We really think you should try this: throw out a horrible idea—with a straight face—and see how your people respond. If nothing else, next time you have an awful idea, they might speak up and call you on it, thinking it's just another test.)

How genuinely curious are you about what your people have to say? Give yourself a grade (A to F). Now go ask your team members to give you a grade (this is a prove-it's-safe exercise as well), but put it this way: "From A to F, how interested do you think I am in what you have to say?" Be curious when you ask.

Who are the introverts and newcomers in your organization? When was the last time one of them spoke up with an idea, suggestion, or critique and what was it?

Notes—Chapter 12

1. **Yahoo! called upon Marisa Mayer...** Mayer's stories about Bruce Springsteen and listening to an employee at a Friday afternoon gathering come from a brief interview at Yahoo! headquarters in September of 2014.
2. **Is the tallest redwood...** Kahneman.
3. **Judges rolling dice...** Kahneman.
4. **Anchoring effect...** Kahneman.
5. **Jeff Bezos, CEO and founder of Amazon...** Brad Stone, *The Everything Store* (New York, NY: Little, Brown and Company, 2013). The account of Project Fargo is found on pages 81-82.
6. **Authentic questions...** I developed a model for asking questions which suggests there are three levels: Yes/No, Spearfishing, and Authentic. The quality of discussion in a classroom results substantially from the level of questioning.
7. **Black and Gold Leadership Forum..** Over the course of its history, the Black and Gold Leadership Forum has heard from Red Auerbach, Mike Krzyzewski, General Norman Schwarzkopf, General David Petraeus, Jack Welch, Lou Gerstner, Jim Collins, Malcolm Gladwell, Elaine Cho, Frances Hesselbein, President George H.W. Bush, Howard Schultz, Jim Sinegal, Ross Perot, Patrick Lencioni, and even visited John Wooden in his home, shortly before he passed away.
8. **Ralph and Cheryl Broetje's apple business...** Matt Kincaid tells the Broetje story based on his PhD dissertation and a follow-up interview with Cheryl Broetje in September, 2014.
9. **General Stanley McChrystal launched Cultural Support teams...** We heard about this concept from a friend—Dan Lao—whose wife served on one of the teams. We sourced further information here: http://www.usnews.com/news/articles/2013/05/16/elite-female-units-may-open-doors-to-special-ops
10. **Our thoughts are shackled...** Jonah Lehrer, *Imagine* (New York, NY: Houghton Mifflin Harcourt, 2012), p. 128.
11. **Everyone dislikes creativity...** Derek Thompson, *The Atlantic*, ibid.

CHAPTER 13: THE PROMISED LAND

So what?

Building a Say Anything culture takes strength. Comfort and isolation are the signs of true weakness.

The Norton Model suggests we all experience an "Ouch" when receiving feedback; then we pass blame. The value unfolds at stage three: "What can I learn from this?"

Employ Schein's cultural embedding mechanisms (role model, reward, pay attentio) to forge a fearless culture. Test it with the Organizational Conversation Killer device.

In the Promised Land, everyone speaks fearlessly, and the results are overwhelmingly positive.

Personal reflection...

When have you felt an "Ouch," and how long did it take to learn something productive from the feedback? What did you learn?

Leadership reflection...

Grade yourself (A to F): can the people you lead Say Anything to you? Now ask them the same question.

Sit down with your team and discuss the grades. As you do so, prove it's safe by diving in first, dignifying every try, and being genuinely curious. Ask Authentic Questions and seek out the introverts and newcomers. Just have a great conversation.

What are the next steps you need to take next to forge a fearless culture?

Notes—Chapter 13

1. **Coach Brown was just ticked off...** interview with Brown, October, 2104. Information about Brown's appearance alongside Scott Waddle came from follow-up emails.
2. **Doe Kittay's customer service organization...** interview with Doe Kittay, October, 2014. Follow-on information about Kittay's experiences at Grainger are from the same interview.
3. **If a basic assumption comes to be strongly held...** Edgar Schein, *Organizational Culture and Leadership*, 4th ed. (San Francisco, CA: Jossey-Bass, 2010), p. 28.
4. **Argues for a similar understanding...** Michael Watkins, "What Is Organizational Culture? And Why Should We Care?" May 15, 2013. See: https://hbr.org/2013/05/what-is-organizational-culture/
5. **To foster or change culture...** Schein, 236.
6. **Our instinctive response to another's critique...** We invented the name "Norton Model" in tribute to Mark Norton, who shared this with me sometime in 2011.
7. **The type of information that gets shared...** Sandra Robinson and Sabrina Deutsch-Salamon, "The Impact of Trust on Organizational Performance," *Human Resource Management Association* (Canada), October 2011, p. 4.
8. **You have to put a lot of nonsense...** Susan Cain, ibid., p. 194.

RECOMMENDED READING
(in order of SAY ANYTHING relevance)

Difficult Conversations
by Stone, Patton, and Heen

Quiet
by Susan Cain

Thirteen Days
by Robert F. Kennedy

Team of Rivals
by Doris Kearns Goodwin

Give and Take
by Adam Grant

Outliers
by Malcolm Gladwell

ACKNOWLEDGMENTS

We can't really think of a time we've read through an acknowledgments section (unless we thought we might be mentioned). So we're keeping it short and doing it differently.

Jennifer Porter

Will you please edit two full iterations, get us in contact with multiple power players, suggest a new subtitle, and basically be responsible for making this the best book possible?

Geoff Webb

Hey Geoff—we know working for the biggest company in the world means you can't help write this book, but you teach this stuff. Could you give us a great idea about an NFL kicker anyway?

Larry Olson and Scott Snook

Will you help me with another book? Please?

Alaina Kincaid

I know we are moving, and I have three other jobs, but just bear with me on this book? Love you. :)

Stephanie Crandall

Steph! Steph! Come listen to what I just wrote. No…right now. Hurry. Love you. :)

Adam Grant

Hi. You don't know me, but I know people who know you, and I've heard you're a giver. Will you look at our book? Endorse it even?

I didn't sleep last night, and I need to write. Be quiet.

John, Jason, Mackenzie, and Timmy Crandall

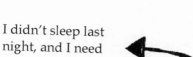

INDEX

Doug Crandall is a graduate of West Point and the Stanford Graduate School of Business. He has led multiple units in the Army, and spent time in operations at Amazon.com. For five years, Doug taught leadership at West Point, where he won the Excellence in Teaching Award and exceeded the academy average in every area of teaching feedback during each semester he taught. He's the co-author of two other books—*Hope Unseen* and *Leadership Lessons from West Point*—and he's written case studies for both Stanford's and Harvard's business schools. He teaches leadership and leader development inside some of the world's most recognizable organizations.

Matt Kincaid holds an MBA and a PhD in Leadership Studies from Gonzaga University. He has led the efforts of three startup companies and worked as a business consultant, managing strategic planning projects for an array of Fortune 500 companies. As a tenured Associate Professor at Columbia Basin College, Matt has been ranked in the top 10% of professors every quarter since joining the institution, with several of his evaluations scoring among the highest in the college's 50+ year history. His work on servant-leadership has been published internationally.

You can learn more about their work with leaders at:
www.bluerudderleadership.com

41787916R00170

Made in the USA
Lexington, KY
27 May 2015